*MAKING
SENSE*

MAKING SENSE

SENSE

The child's construction of the world

Edited by
Jerome Bruner and
Helen Haste

METHUEN
London and New York

First published in 1987 by
Methuen & Co. Ltd
11 New Fetter Lane, London EC4P 4EE

Published in the USA by
Methuen & Co.
in association with Methuen, Inc.
29 West 35th Street,
New York, NY 10001

Typeset by MC Typeset Ltd,
Chatham, Kent
Printed in Great Britain by
Richard Clay Ltd, Bungay, Suffolk

*British Library Cataloguing in
Publication Data*

Making sense: the child's construction of the world
    1. Interpersonal   communication
in children
I. Bruner, Jerome S. II. Weinreich-
Haste, Helen
155.4'13   BF723.C57

ISBN 0-416-38240-1
ISBN 0-416-92490-5 Pbk

*Library of Congress Cataloging in
Publication Data*

Making Sense
    Bibliography: P.
    Includes indexes.
    1. Child psychology. 2. Social in-
teraction in children. 3. Problem
solving in children. 4. Children—
language.   I. Bruner,   Jerome
Seymour.   II. Weinreich-Haste,
Helen.
BF721.M215   1987   155.4
87-11153

ISBN 0-416-38240-1
ISBN 0-416-92490-5

Contents

Contributors

ANN L. BROWN is Professor of Psychology, University of Illinois.

JEROME BRUNER is George Herbert Mead University Professor, New School for Social Research, New York.

GEORGE BUTTERWORTH is Professor of Psychology, University of Stirling.

JUDY S. DELOACHE teaches at the Department of Human Development and Family Ecology, University of Illinois.

MARGARET DONALDSON is Emeritus Professor of Developmental Psychology, University of Edinburgh.

JUDY DUNN is Professor of Human Development, The Pennsylvania State University.

CAROL FLEISHER FELDMAN is Professor of Psychology, New York University and Cuny Graduate Center.

HELEN HASTE is Senior Lecturer in Psychology, University of Bath.

PAUL LIGHT is Senior Lecturer in Psychology, University of Southampton.

BARBARA LLOYD is Reader in Psychology in the School of Social Sciences, University of Sussex.

Acknowledgements

The editors and publishers would like to thank the following for their kind permission to reproduce copyright material. Chapter 4 is reprinted by permission of the publishers from *Actual Minds, Possible Worlds*, by Jerome S. Bruner, Cambridge, Massachusetts: Harvard University Press, copyright © 1986 by the President and Fellows of Harvard College. Figure 9.1 from 'Morality, social meaning and rhetoric, the social context of moral reasoning', in *Morality, Moral Behaviour and Moral Development*, edited by W. Kurtines and J. Gewirtz, copyright © 1984 Helen Weinreich Haste, is reprinted by permission of John Wiley & Sons, Inc. Figure 9.2 from *Beyond Universals in Cognitive Development* by D.H. Feldman, copyright © 1980 is reprinted by permission of Ablex Publishing Corporation.

Introduction

JEROME BRUNER

and HELEN HASTE

A quiet revolution has taken place in developmental psychology in the last decade. It is not only that we have begun to think again of the child as a *social being* – one who plays and talks with others, learns through interactions with parents and teachers – but because we have come once more to appreciate that through such social life, the child acquires a framework for interpreting experience, and learns how to negotiate meaning in a manner congruent with the requirements of the culture. 'Making sense' is a social process; it is an activity that is always situated within a cultural and historical context.

Before that, we had fallen into the habit of thinking of the child as an 'active scientist', constructing hypotheses about the world, reflecting upon experience, interacting with the physical environment and formulating increasingly complex structures of thought. But this active, constructing child had been conceived as a rather isolated being, working alone at her problem-solving. Increasingly we see now that, given an appropriate, shared social context, the child seems more competent as an intelligent social operator than she is as a 'lone scientist' coping with a world of unknowns. Hughes and Donaldson showed in their classic study, for example, that a child who cannot take another's perspective in the Piagietian three-mountains test can nevertheless 'hide the boy from the policeman' in a socially realistic task, though the two tests are formally identical. Or to take another case, though the young child is highly egocentric on tasks involving abstract space or time, she can empathize with the feeling of her siblings and master the 'shifting' personal pronouns of her language.

But the issue does not hinge on early competence; it inheres, rather, in a recognition of the significance of *language* in mental development. The child's use of language rests on her ability to appreciate the perspective of others – that *you* mean *you* when you say *I*, and *I* mean *I* when I say it, which involves a working understanding of reciprocal relations. In relations with others the child early has the capacity to negotiate meaning and to interpret what is going on – even before her full powers of lexico-grammatical speech have matured. Through language, the child is quickly aided in her entry into *culture*: its metaphors, its kinds of explanation, its categories, and its ways of interpreting and evaluating events. These are not *invented* by the child; they are the common currency of the culture, the framework that determines the boundaries of the child's concepts. Its medium is language and the forms of linguistic behaviour.

The chapters in this book draw on a range of research studies that reflect this emerging perspective. They explore four themes: the construction of a *methodology* suitable to the new emphasis in developmental studies; revisions of the idea of the child as *competent* and *self-regulating*; the nature of the 'social representations' that provide the frames for interpreting culture; and, finally, a reappraisal of the *role of language* and discourse in the development of the child's schemas for interpreting experience. A word about each is in order.

About *methodology*, the chief issue is the nature of the settings in which we observe (or 'experiment' with) the signs of growth in the developing child. This includes, of course, the kinds of 'materials' and 'instructions' that we provide the child to play or work with while we observe her. The tendency in the past has been to contrive highly 'controlled' situations involving unfamiliar or 'new' material with which the child has had little experience. This is very much in keeping with the old interpretation of the child as a little scientist, interpreting the world on her own. The new emphasis, instead, places the child in a normally complex situation and then observes the child's ordinary efforts to cope with it – to assign an interpretion to the situation that is congruent with her intention and that takes account of the role of others in the situation.

As an illustration, consider a 10-minute incident that involved one of us, a friend of hers, and his daughter, Sophie (2 years, 7 months).

> At first, Sophie sat on her father's knee while he attempted to talk to me. She tried to attract his attention by addressing remarks to him and by pulling at him. Eventually she paused; 'want to do a poo'. She looked expectantly at both her father and me in turn. I suggested to her father that she might be taken upstairs; he repied that she was expressing boredom rather than a biological need, and to her he said, 'No, you can wait until we go home, it won't be long.' I then found a nest of Russian dolls. She assembled one small doll and placed it inside a much larger one, which she closed; she then did the same thing with two others. She clearly understood the task, though was not able to assemble the dolls in systematic sequence. Throughout she maintained a commentary on what she was doing, trying to correct her mistakes both in action and in her commentary. While she was doing this her father interspersed his ongoing conversation with me, with comments on Sophie's activities and suggestions to her about what she might do next, and encouraging her efforts.

This incident is typical of a thousand such in the child's life (rather more typical than the idyllically undistracted parent–child communication usually observed by psychologists). The presence of a second adult divides the parent's attention and makes the child a witness to their conversational commentary on her own behaviour and as well as whatever else the adults are discussing. This interweaves with her own direct interaction with the parent and with his commentary on her own behaviour. The incident has many interesting features. Firstly, it is clear that Sophie is very competent in understanding social interaction. She tried several strategies to gain the adults' attention, and when she produced her *coup de grâce*, she clearly appreciated its impact.

Like the children described by Judy Dunn in Chapter 1 and Carol Feldman in Chapter 7, Sophie is capable of dissembling and manipulating her physical and psychological states, and she expects that her actions will be interpreted and commented upon by her father. In the first part of the interaction, the underlying 'game' she was playing might be described as 'Daddy is working and doesn't want to be distracted; how do I do it?' Her father's comment on her effective strategy, ascribing it to boredom, defined the situation as being such a game and dissimulation. Parent and child were effectively colluding in defining her plea for attention. The event represented the social definition of a linguistic act which did not focus on what was actually said, but the reason for saying it.

In the second part of the interaction, when Sophie was playing with the dolls, her father's comments served to affirm her definition of the task (to assemble the dolls in sequence) and to endorse and affirm her own commentary on her performance. What he said scaffolded her concept of the task and of the strategies needed to perform the task properly; it also affirmed that her activity was valued and one expected of children. She also appreciated the *ad rem* nature of this form of communication and used her father's advice appropriately.

This brief vignette provides a picture of a child in a social world, a world where language, interaction and cognition are interwoven. It illustrates the role of developing intersubjective meaning, of the negotiation of an intersubjective interpretation of what is going on. Sophie is learning how to handle possible explanations and possible goals, and how to evaluate and understand an 'overall script' (Daddy working, Sophie bored, Sophie achieving a task).

The illustration we have chosen makes clear, we hope, the importance of our interpretative approach to the child's behaviour. This is what lies at the heart of much of the newer methodology: something akin to what the anthropologist Clifford Geertz refers to as 'thick interpretation'. To understand what the child is doing, one needs to observe her efforts to cope with a familiar, contextually rich task in which she is, so to speak, 'holding up her own end' of things.

This leads directly to the second emphasis in the chapters that follows: a revised conception of *competence* and *self-regulation*. Because of the 'quiet revolution', we can see Sophie's behaviour and that of her father and friend as an integral process. Her development depends not upon her constantly reinventing the wheel, but upon her capacity to integrate her needs and strategies and interpretation with those of significant others around her.

This stress upon the *dialectical* relationship between the individual and the social represents the joining of several strands of thinking from several disciplines. One source is in the work of Vygotsky. It is only in recent years that his much more extensive views about the relationship between individual development and sociohistorical evolution have been appreciated. For him, the child's development depends upon her using, so to speak, the tool kit of the culture to express the powers of mind. Sensitivity to Vygotsky's genius has been furnished by several developments in the present decade.

One development came from sociology. In the late 1960s, writing as sociologists but drawing also upon anthropology, Berger and Luckmann described 'the social construction of reality'. For them, the child makes sense of the culture in which she or he is reared, coming to appreciate the commonsense knowledge which is available within the culture. This commonsense knowledge is expressed directly through language in the form of rules, but even more extensively through the style and use of language, the selection of categories deemed appropriate for classifying different behaviours, and forms of address which communicate and reproduce the relations between persons of differing ranks and roles. Language *objectifies* reality and makes possible the transmission of meaning (and its evaluation) across generations who share common concepts. It is through language that meanings and concepts are reproduced and made enduring, and it is also through language that such meanings and concepts are modified or replaced, in response to social change.

Many anthropologists have also shifted from observing the structure of the social world in terms of static and formal kinship or economic relations, and are now looking at how culture is manifested in the structure of behaviour, in language and in non-verbal communication. They are exploring the meaning that interactions have, and the ways by which the meaning and symbols of interaction are reinforced and reproduced. According to this approach, interactions reflect the *enactment* of shared interpretations and common symbolic representations about events, relationships and goals. Such 'social facts' *reflect* and also *generate* the framework within which individual experience is interpreted. We have already mentioned Clifford Geertz as an example of this trend.

In Chapter 4, for example, Jerome Bruner discusses the ways in which the distinction between 'public' and 'private' is very much a matter of culture; different cultures have different boundaries, and such boundaries are set and defined in a variety of ways. For example, forms of address express distance in status and in intimacy; physical signs such as fences, closed doors and explicit markings of territory indicate both the shared convention, and the shared means of communication, to define private space. The public–private distinction is also revealed through language, the content of what is spoken about, what is not said, and to whom.

Another example of a social fact is gender. In Chapter 9, Helen Haste describes Bourdieu's analysis of the ways in which gender boundaries are expressed in a culture. It is through greeting forms, through the delineation of certain places as 'female' and certain as 'male', through clothing and stance. It is also through metaphor: the idea of 'brother sun, sister moon', and of male as light and female as dark, of male as hard and female as soft. All these symbols and behaviours signal that gender is a highly significant social category; the definitions and signs of gender differentiation are embedded within the language, and in the practical action, of a culture.

The study of frames of meaning, and how language not only *expresses* but *circumscribes* the ways in which experience is to be interpreted, is also reflected in cross-cultural psychology. For a long period many cross-cultural psychologists seemed preoccupied with comparative studies of performance – testing the relative speed of progression through stages of development. Now attention has shifted to looking at how cultural frames of meaning shape the perception and conception of the child, and indeed how cultural symbols reflect *which* frameworks, schemas and scripts are transmitted to the child.

Within psychology, we can trace several separate developments – indeed, they are in some ways so separate that they have at times seemed to be in conflict. From psycholinguistics has come the realization that there is more to language than speech facility, and that the child is able to express concepts not only by what is said – the content – but by the form of words used. As Bruner argues in Chapter 4, the child shows extraordinary sophistication in using deictic shifters – the realization that if I say 'you' and 'here', you the observer must use the expressions 'I' and 'there' to reflect the same event; this illustrates both a conceptual ability, and also something which is inherent in the structure of the language. The linguistic form *represents* reference and mutuality between persons, yet at the same time the child is able to handle these concepts at a prelinguistic level. So language is constitutive of meaning, yet the child also has the latent capacity to deal in the concepts before she has the linguistic forms.

Another strand comes from social psychology. Social psychologists have demonstrated the ways in which social categories are defined and evaluated by the use of commonly available images and explanations. For example, Tajfel and his associates created artificial and ephemeral 'groups' in laboratory settings, and found that this was sufficient to evoke complex linguistic categories by which the 'ingroup' was positively described and evaluated, and the outgroup was negatively described and evaluated. A linguistic-cognitive distinction – 'our group' versus 'them' – could set up severe social consequences in the real world. And the distinction is easily transmitted to the developing child. All of this made it plain that notions like competence and self-regulation were not to be accounted for by invoking the growth of autonomous cognitive structures. What provides the 'clout' to developing cognitive structure, as Vygotsky early told us, was the extent to which it enabled the growth child to use the instruments of language and culture. But Vygotsky raised an anomaly: the instruments of language and culture also promote the growth of individual mental structures.

This brings us directly to the third emphasis in the chapters that follow: the nature and role of *social representations*. Work on language and culture suggests that subgroups within a culture generate a set of schemas or frameworks (including theories about their origins and functions) which identify them as an ingroup, and assign outgroup status to other groups. Such theories, and the vocabulary and concepts arising from them, come to permeate the culture and to shape the ways in which people construct their experience. Moscovici for example has examined how social representations provide a framework or theory for the interpretation of experience. Similarly Breakwell, and Williams and Giles have shown how the social changes arising from the feminist movement are accompanied by, and reified by, new ways of representing 'male' and 'female' as social groups, the relationship between men and women, and the descriptions of 'masculinity' and 'femininity'. The emergence or creation of a new social representation in response to social change reflects a changing concept, but also makes it possible for the concept to be available to a wider society.

In keeping with these new trends, many developmental psychologists have come to criticize the picture of the lone child which they consider to underlie the orthodox Piagetian model. A number of researchers have demonstrated the importance of collaborative acitvity in enhancing problem-solving ability. They have observed the role of language and interaction in exploring possible solutions. What in fact happens in such interactions is that the child's own cognitive approach to the problem is challenged, either by peers directly or by parents or teachers 'scaffolding' understanding through pacing of the problem-solving process. These observations have moved developmental psychologists to give much more weight to interaction with others, and to the use of language, in the growth of concepts and the developing structure of mind. At the very least, the child's development must be mediated by, and stimulated by, interaction with others.

It is this climate of increasing appreciation of social and linguistic processes that has fuelled a renewal of interest in Vygotsky's work. We now begin to understand more clearly what he intended by his famous dictum:

> Any function in the child's cultural development appears twice, or on two planes. First it appears on the social plane, and then on the psychological plane. First it appears between people as an interpsychological category, and then within the child as an intrapsychological category. This is equally true with regard to voluntary attention, logical memory, and

the formation of concepts, and the development of volition.

But perhaps even more revolutionary for developmental psychologists, and reflecting an understanding of cultural processes, is Vygotsky's view that language is a *symbol system* which reflects sociohistorical development. Thus the set of frameworks for interpretation available to the growing individual reflects the *organizing consciousness of the whole culture* – in other words it is difficult, if not impossible, for a child to develop a concept that does not have an expression within her culture of origin, either specifically in language or within other means by which communication is enacted. It follows from this that the development of concepts will depend on the available resources within the culture: the mnemonic systems available to the child will affect how she develops codes for remembering; the mathematical systems will influence how the child acquires abstract mathematical thinking as well as how she learns a counting system in the first place.

However, there are some important differences between Vygotsky and the current orientations within both developmental and social psychology. It is of significance that for a long time the major impact of Vygotsky's work in development psychology was confined to his perceived 'dispute' with Piaget over the extent to which concepts required language for their formation. To a large extent, this issue was discussed within the context of the individual child's competence and development; it was not seen in terms of the social or interactive dimensions of language. Until recently, the main impact of Vygotsky's ideas of empirical research has been the concept of the 'zone of proximal development', the gap between what the child can currently do, given the constraints of her cognitive functioning, and what she can achieve with the intercession and scaffolding of adults or peers. One might argue that the enthusiasm for the concept arises partly from the fact that it is easily researchable. More to the point, perhaps, it is congruent with the classical theoretical and methodological preoccupations of Western developmental psychologists. That is to say, the ZPD 'adds' something to development which can still be seen as a solo, autonomous process. Developmental psychologists, as a community, still do not really appreciate the wider social, cultural and historical dimensions of Vygotsky's theoretical framework, translating 'social' only into 'interpersonal', not into 'sociohistorical' or 'cultural'.

In contrast, social psychologists have, generally, recognized many of the ideas implied in the 'sociohistorical perspective' of Vygotsky in their appreciation of such concepts as 'social representations', but have failed to cite Vygotsky and, furthermore, have omitted any analysis of processes of development which might take account of qualitative changes in the child's understanding. In Harré's sensitive accounts of how the child learns the ways to be effective in using the symbols, signs and appropriate interactive behaviours of her culture, both in communicating and in being seen as a 'proper' member of society, for example, there is little or no attention paid to the mechanisms of individual development, internalization, or recognition that there may be progressive change in the qualitative structure of the child's understanding. Only recently has there begun research on the *developmental* parameters of social representations.

In sum, it is probably a reasonable generalization to say that until recently developmental psychologists have not escaped from the implicit assumption that the child comes to understand some 'universals' through a gradually evolving cognitive structure. This ontogenesis is assisted by others providing concepts through language, and stimulation to growth through interaction. In contrast, social psychologists and sociologists have behaved largely as if the world is constructed by groups within cultures, who create frameworks for consciousness and the interpretation of experiences which rely on common shared symbols and representations. The child is *inserted* into these frameworks through learning how to use the symbols and how to interpret the representations.

This brings us to the fourth theme that emerges in the chapters that follow. It concerns *the role of language and discourse* in development. We have already commented upon related matters *en passant*, but we can now be more explicit. To do so we must first say a few words by way of background.

It was typical of work on 'language and thought' in the 1970s that one looked for concordances between stages of cognitive development and the mastery of certain linguistic forms – principally syntactic or semantic forms. The guiding image was rather a static one, relating to the acquisition of certain definite cognitive and certain definite linguistic capacities. Does achievement of the 'concept of the object' (in the Piagetian sense) correspond in some way to achievement of steady and standard lexical forms? The issue could then be argued as to whether one 'led' to the other, whether they were autonomous developments, etc. Research along these lines led to a great deal of research, much of it rather inconclusive; it was based, in the main, on a capacity or competence model of mind – the successive appearance of different cognitive and linguistic competences being taken for granted. The variability introduced by situation and context was what finally discouraged such efforts at correlation.

The emphasis over the last decade has shifted away from concern with syntax and semantics, and with stages of development, towards an understanding of the role of discourse and dialogic processes. How does language interaction serve to 'scaffold' the child's efforts at expressing and understanding both events and utterances? How are categories, explanations and representations embodied in interactive discourse? How are underlying intentions of the speaker expressed and interpreted in discourse? How do concepts of interaction in general become embodied in linguistic exchanges? Questions of this order are well represented in the chapters that follow. When we turn to them we see striking instances of these four emphases.

Consider two consequences of the shift in methodology. The first is that one can now appreciate the actual *competence* of the child, which is greater than had been believed. The second is that we are now able to focus on the child as a *social being* whose competences are interwoven with the competences of others. In Chapter 1 Judy Dunn describes her studies of children's behaviour with siblings. She points out that inferring role-taking ability from verbal exercises is problematic, but that observation of children's actual behaviour with peers reveals a complex capacity for role-taking, taking the part of the other. Three-year-olds are skilful in reading and in anticipating their younger siblings' reactions, and even younger children, around fifteen months, can tease, provoke and comfort others – an ability which is the enactment of quite complex role-taking. That can be ascertained only in 'natural' situations. Around two years, children can simulate emotion, both in interaction with others and in pretend play. Margaret Donaldson, in Chapter 5, shows how the child's ordinary conversation reveals subtle conceptual understanding; Laura, aged 2 years, 10 months, shows that when an action is proposed (going unstairs) she can entertain the possibility of an alternative action, the antithesis of the one suggested (going downstairs). Traditional methodologies would not easily tap such complex inferences being drawn by a child of that age; they are evident in ordinary language, but not easily manipulated in an experimental setting.

Paul Light, in Chapter 2, also shows that in situations that are personally meaningful, the child reveals subtle understanding. He points out that the problems surrounding children's performance in the three-mountains test are not a matter of whether the child can take the role of the other, but are complicated by the fact that the child is operating from the 'best vantage point'; thus the child is taking *a point of view*, but not the point of view of a particular other person. Children who cannot resolve the three-mountains problem can nevertheless predict what the 'other' will see when presented with two-sided pictures. Similarly, children under 7 can appreciate what the various characters in a story can understand about each other, though they cannot differentiate the privileged knowledge of the reader from what is known by the characters. Light also makes the striking point that role-taking is something that children can do long before they are able to articulate it – which is consistent, he argues, with Mead's view that role-taking is *implicit* in social behaviour rather than *underlying* it.

Such extensive evidence of the precocity of the child's actual role-taking skills indicates the methodological developments which these chapters illustrate. But it also requires us to confront some of the definitions we use. In Chapter 3, George Butterworth argues that we need to reconstruct the concept of *egocentrism* and redefine what 'role' and 'perspective-taking' may mean in different contexts. He criticizes the limitations of Piaget's constructivist perspective, which places so much stress on action or on the operation of the intellect. This, he argues, implies that perceptual and perspective-taking competence require *representation*; the evidence suggests a more direct access for perception. His own experiments on babies' perspective-taking show that babies adjust their own line of gaze to that of the mother; they can interpret the perspective of the mother's perception and act accordingly. Such evidence casts doubt on Piaget's picture of the child's egocentrism.

Changing methodology has also highlighted problems of theory concerning the child's competence. We see increasing evidence for a 'competent infant' when the infant is allowed to define the task, set the goal, and respond to the demands of the task on her own terms. But Judy DeLoache and Ann Brown, in Chapter 6, warn against an *over*emphasis on the competence of young children, an overreaction to minimizing their competence and self-directiveness in previous research. They describe how ingenious and inventive young children are in defining a variety of tasks, in directing their own activities with a high degree of motivation, and in correcting their errors. They found that children even attempt to develop a *principle* of task solution; in a balancing task with weighted blocks, for example, they not only looked for a principle, but memorized a large amount of material and devised their own strategies for proceeding – consistent with the model of 'the child as scientist'.

DeLoache and Brown also show that children are much more involved in the task, and more competent in devising and using strategies, when they work on problems that they themselves have set. Hitherto, research on children's problem-solving has tended to focus on what they could *not* do, rather than what they *could*. DeLoache and Brown's work focuses instead on the familiar activities of children's everyday life where they are often able to do more than is usually expected of them. Their work contributes to a theoretical model of the child as self-initiating and self-directing, but also has important methodological implications for how we conduct research on young children.

The evidence for the child's self-direction comes from other chapters as well. Both Bruner and Donaldson describe how children of 1 year, as yet unable to verbalize – or even to have verbal concepts – can resolve conflicts of choice that involve

holding two objects in mind simultaneously. To resolve such
conflicts, the child must have some concept of alternative
actions, and must have some strategy of choice. For example,
the child comes to a door with her hands full. She cannot open
it. She may drop the held objects and try to retrieve them. But
eventually the child will put the objects down, open the door
and pick up the objects again. Sequencing such complex
actions, once thought to be out of the young child's reach, is
well within her competence given a familiar situation and
enough time to cope with it.

These examples exhibit a common theme: when the child
defines a problem for herself, or has a self-generated intention
that requires overcoming an intervening obstacle, her mode of
coping is far more integrated than when she has a problem and
an intention imposed on her by the experimenter. Her
strategies for attaining her own goals show typical trial and
error, self-correction, and a sensitivity to alternative strategies.
She eventually acquires a repertoire of strategies that can be
applied in a variety of situations, and this is greatly aided when
she is able to represent these symbolically and through
language. But it is in the early stages of development, when
strategies are gradually being developed, that the role of
self-direction and initiative are particularly interesting. These
strategies do not emerge full-blown. There is a sequence in
their emergence. To begin with, strategies are task-specific, and
then become generalized. Qualitatively, the stages of strategy
can be characterized roughly as *brute force, local correction,
taking it apart and starting again*, and, finally, *viewing the effort as
a whole*. These stages reflect a developmental model developed
by Karmiloff-Smith, central to which is the idea of *theory-in-
action*. The child's theory-in-action is, Karmiloff-Smith suggests, a key issue in understanding the child's motivation,
persistence and capacity for endless self-correction in the face of
setback and frustration. The child's efforts are eventually
greatly strengthened by the use of language for representing
intention and sequence.

Language, of course, is a major theme of this volume. The
recognition of its constitutive role in cognition rests not only on
its power to differentiate concepts, but on its power to give
'ontic' status to concepts and to make them accessible for

transmission as part of culture. But this involves more than syntax and semantics.

As Bruner notes in Chapter 4, there is more to communicating meaning than the content of what is said; there are *illocutionary* features by which a speaker's intentions are transmitted and by which a speaker makes clear his or her interpretation of the context in which communication is occurring. Even very young children become very adept at 'reading' the intentions of a speaker's utterance, even when it does not literally correspond to the conventional content of the message as spoken.

A similar point is made by Margaret Donaldson in Chapter 5. She examines the idea that language is *embedded*. We make sense of what people mean because we have access to a wide range of cues that tell us what is the context, what is the problem to which the speaker is referring. Gestures and movements of the speaker direct us to the particular context. Such non-linguistic clues, as Bruner points out, also give us information about the degree of importance of what is being said. The embeddedness of speech in a communicative context is something we take for granted; we do not realize that we are not relying simply on the meanings of words put together in a grammatical way. As various writers have indicated, however much the structure of language communicates about meaning, in ordinary interactions we rely greatly on other information. Indeed, it is because speech and thought are usually embedded that the young child is able to engage in apparently complex logical exercises – such as negation – which are way beyond her if presented in disembedded language.

Donaldson sees this as accounting in part for the gap between what a child can do in a real-life problem-solving setting, and what she can do – or cannot do – when the same problem is presented in more remote terms. In many settings, however, we are forced to consider what words mean, since they are not always contextually embedded. In practice, of course, we do not simply listen to the words and derive their meaning from these alone. We try to make sense of them by treating them to memory, knowledge and association. We make them 'mean' by locating them in our known world. In some situations remote from our own lives, however, we do have to 'make sense' of the isolated meaning of utterances. Donaldson notes that trying to couch unfamiliar or ambiguous material in a familiar context may be highly misleading. And this poses very difficult problems for adult and child alike. To couch such unfamiliar or ambiguous material to the child in seemingly familiar or universal terms may result in invoking misleading associations and misleading interpretations in the child's mind. The communicative task, where children are the recipients, is not simply a matter of making things familiar by the use of comprehensible language, but of ensuring that the correct association or interpretive resonance is evoked. For meaning, as Frege assured us many years ago, involves both sense and reference, and the former depends upon far more than a knowledge of the lexicon.

In Chapter 7, Carol Feldman distinguishes between the *epistemic* and the *ontic*, in both cognition and language. This is a distinction between 'old' and 'new' knowledge, and there are different requirements involved in operating upon each. The epistemic aspect of knowing is *coming to know*, the operation of mental acts upon the world; the ontic is the means by which the situation is *construed and represented*, made 'reality'. Making something real, giving it ontological status, requires the creation or evocation of a form of representation; this creates a concept so that what was 'new' and to be operated upon now becomes 'old', 'given' or taken for granted. She calls this process 'ontic dumping'. Essentially, the process of ontic dumping is the means by which a rule or a strategy for solving a particular problem becomes a rule-in-itself for application in any appropriate context; it becomes a concept *about* knowing, rather than a *route to* knowing in a particular case.

The child or adult, however, does not create the representations and symbols for transforming the epistemic to the ontic *ab initio*. As other chapters in this volume express in different ways, the individual draws on existing categories to create ontic dumps. It is through language that the process occurs; language encodes representations of strategies, rules and stipulations, and makes possible the exchange of 'created realities' between persons within a culture. An epistemic act, when it is finally 'dumped' into ontic status and embodied in language, becomes a part of the transmissible culture, part of the tool kit for representing concepts, strategies and the like.

All of this highlights the importance of the dialectic between the child's own thinking and her immediate social world, represented in language and shared concepts. But what of that broader cultural world? What aspects of it are available to the child? Earlier we discussed two models for explicating the construction of meaning at the cultural level. One was the work of Moscovici and the 'French School' of social psychology, which posits ways in which social groups either construct or disseminate symbolic representations of the world, and frameworks for its interpretation. But though it is a useful model, it has little to say about the actual processes by which the child acquires cultural knowledge.

The second model, Vygotsky's, provides a better account of the process of acquisition while at the same time keeping in mind the role of sociohistorical evolution. For Vygotsky sees the culture changing through the accretion of concepts and representations that emerge historically – changes that, so to speak, reflect the plight of individuals living in a communal culture. Over historical time, this changed store of cultural representations affects the dialogue into which the child enters as he grows up. 'Ways of thought' becomes embedded in the culture not only as its science, its literature and art, and its ideology, but also as its 'common sense'. Central to Vygotsky's theory is the principle that concepts are first acquired by the child 'externally', in dialogue, and then become internalized to elaborate and differentiate thought.

This essentially Vygotskyian idea is picked up in several chapters in this volume. In Chapter 8 Barbara Lloyd explores the ways in which the social representations of gender are transmitted to the child. Gender is a primary social category: it is highly salient in adult interactions, and it is marked in a wide variety of behaviours, including presentations of self, forms of behaviour, modes of address and styles of interaction. It also carries with it implicit theories about the nature, function and origin of gender differences. These constitute the accepted justifications for maintaining and reproducing the social category. The symbols of gender are with us in all fields of life, and the representation of gender is enacted in practically all our interactions. While all societies apparently have gender as a salient category, they differ in the forms the symbols take, and in the degree to which gender categories permeate social and personal life.

Lloyd concentrates on the ways in which British children encounter and internalize social representations of gender. She observes that mothers reflect their own representations of gender in the way that they respond to children even at the age of 6 months, both by actions (the toys they give the child) and through language (what is said, the adjectives used to describe the child, and the style of linguistic interaction). Thus, in their own behaviour and use of symbols, they reveal their own representations; by enacting them in a variety of ways, the mother scaffolds the child's interpretation of his or her experience in such a way as to provide a framework in which gender is highly salient, and which ensures that boys have a different framework for interpreting experience than girls. By 13 months, boys and girls behave differently: they are effectively operating in their different representational schemes.

In Chapter 9, Helen Haste looks at the child's encounters with a variety of systems of rules for interpreting experience. She uses three examples; rules for moral and conventional behaviour, rules for making maps, and rules for conceptualizing the distinction between health and illness. These are 'rules' in the sense that there is a cultural *grammar* for the interpretative process. Through practice and action, and through schemas provided by adults and peers, the child grows into understanding the representations and symbols of the culture. For example, the culture distinguishes 'moral' and 'conventional' rules; the child experiences this distinction in the ways that adults behave in response to different transgressions. The child herself behaves differently; she invokes different kinds of sanctions and different metaphors, in response to moral and conventional transgressions. How we define a person as 'ill' also depends on a vast array of assumptions about social roles and the expectations of their normal competent performance. To be defined socially as 'ill' requires the reciprocal behaviour of a range of people, which differs significantly from their normal roles. The child acquires these concepts and actions through her own illnesses, and by observing those of people close to her. Furthermore, 'being ill' involves theories about the causes and cures of sickness. Much has been written about cultural variations in explanations of illness, and in particular about the moral dimension of becoming ill and becoming better. Illness is a particularly good example of the interweaving of language, linguistic behaviour, symbols and narrative in social representations, and of the way that the child comes to frame her own experience in terms of such representations. Haste, like Lloyd, shows how the stages of children's cognitive growth develop within the framework of social representations and symbols. This illustrates, again, the Vygotskian dialectic between the social world and individual development.

In Chapter 4, Bruner refers to another aspect of social representation, the stories and narratives which all cultures provide as guidelines for appropriate behaviour. Such stories are not simply 'moral tales', spelling out that a particular act is 'right' or 'wrong'. They tell the growing child (and confirm for the adult) a whole set of parameters about characters, settings and actions that are to be expected in a particular context, and they carry with them the message that such parameters are those which are possible *and comprehensible* within the culture.

But Bruner does not only speak of the more formalized 'stories' of the culture which transmit such frameworks; he also describes the act of making up stories at the informal level, the kinds of accounts of what he terms 'characteristic cultural dramas' which underline possible roles, actions and self-definitions. This goes on, in some sense, in every social interaction where there are comments (both linguistic and paralinguistic) upon the legitimacy and comprehensibility of the child's behaviour. In our earlier example, in giving his account of why Sophie demanded to go to the lavatory, Sophie's father was telling a story about the little drama that was going on, making a coherent narrative which both explained and set the limits of legitimation to Sophie's behaviour and her choice of distracting strategy. In several chapters of the book (Dunn, Feldman, Haste) there are verbatim extracts of children's talk which show children, or child and adult, collaborating in retelling – or creating – a story about what is going on which locates the events in a context that makes sense of it, and affirms the legitimacy and illegitimacy of behaviours. In some cases the examples are of children *enacting* the drama which has its roots in a 'story': Judy Dunn describes the actions of children giving succour to hurt siblings in a way which clearly shows knowledge of the 'script' for soothing hurt. In the example that Helen Haste quotes from William Damon's work, of children negotiating how they will share the reward of candy bars, it is clear that behind the negotiation process lies a variety of 'scripts' or stories about how the exercise should be conducted, about the importance of 'fairness' and what 'fairness' means in such a context. The 'script' for sharing which is being narrated in words and in behaviour by these children includes words like 'fair', 'nice' and 'deserves'. It does *not* include having a physical battle to decide on winners and losers, nor does it include letting the grownup make the decision. Yet these alternative scripts for resolving a problem of sharing do exist within the culture of these children, and would be comprehensible, and legitimated by an appropriate account, had they been invoked.

A final theme of this volume recurs in some form in practically every chapter. It is the question of *discourse*, the interactions between child and peers, but especially between child and parent. The child's most immediate social connections provide the mechanisms for the development of cognition and the acquisition of concepts in Vygotsky's sense. In such interaction the several functions of language and paralinguistic behaviour are most manifest; by focusing on the details of discourse behaviour we can observe the key processes of development.

However, as we have already indicated, though everyone may agree on the significance of discourse, people come to its analysis from different theoretical perspectives. In an earlier part of this discussion, we made a distinction between different psychologists' orientations to individual development. Some see the interaction between the child and others mainly as *facilitating* individual development. This facilitation process is conceived in two ways, as the adult scaffolding the child's struggles to make sense of experience, and as the adult giving the child a set of grammars and scripts for making sense, either directly or through the ways in which the child's own behaviours and utterances are afforded legitimacy. In these conceptualizations of discourse, the parent–child dyad is the major focus of study.

The second orientation is more towards the social and cultural; the child's discourse with the adult is seen as a microcosm of a more extensive social process. The child's individual development is understood in dialectical relation to the parent's own construction of the world and of frames of meaning, and to the wider cultural framework of which the parent is a part. So within this perspective, the uses of language for providing a framework for the child's thinking and experience, and the uses of language as reflecting and reproducing the accounts, stories, symbols, representations and legitimation process of the culture, are of equal interest.

The distinction between these two perspectives is now at last being bridged, and this represents a major advance in psychology. As we indicated earlier, the tradition of developmental psychology has tended to ignore (or take as given and unproblematic) the social context in which development takes place; in contrast, the traditions of social psychology and social anthropology have focused mainly on the social context, and regarded as unproblematic the processes of individual growth into the culture. The greater attention to language in its wider sense has brought these two camps closer together. It is in this process of confluence that Vygotsky's insights into the individual–social dialectic have become so salient. The contributors to this volume reflect different aspects of this rapprochement, and the ways in which they discuss discourse illustrate different parts of the montage.

We can trace three themes in relation to discourse. The first is discourse as *scaffolding*, the second is discourse as the *negotiation of meaning*, and the third is discourse as the *transfer of cultural representations*. They are not mutually exclusive; the parent scaffolding the child's concept of competing successfully at draughts also passes on to the child the cultural value of winning a game.

Judy Dunn, in Chapter 1, shows how older siblings scaffold younger in learning about emotional states – including learning how to tease and annoy, as well as how to comfort and console. She also describes how mothers discuss and structure the feeling states of the child, thus providing a framework for the child's interpretation. Indeed, so powerful is this process in assisting development that Dunn found that by 2 years girls were talking more about feeling states than were boys; half a year earlier it was apparent that mothers talked more to daughters than to sons about feelings. Those children were being scaffolded in *conversation*, which is a manifestation of social intelligence that reflects the child's ability to understand the feeling states of others, and to show interest in the lives and activities of other people.

Both Paul Light and George Butterworth, in Chapters 2 and 3, describe the early scaffolding processes by which the child's interactions with the mother – whether verbal or not – are an important aid in the child's growing ability to take the other's perspective. Through such interactions the child learns, firstly, to attend to the mother's direction of interest and, later, the necessary interactive skill of turn-taking. Barbara Lloyd describes in Chapter 8 the scaffolding by mothers of the child's use of gender-marked language, helping the child to acquire the social classification of toys and behaviour by gender. In Chapter 9, Helen Haste quotes a teacher elaborating a child's explanation of why she was absent from school the day before: effectively the teacher is giving the child a *repertoire* to account acceptably for absence from school.

As we can see, the process of discourse as scaffolding can take general forms: correcting the child's early utterances (as Bruner describes); pacing the child's problem-solving efforts, by responding to the child's ongoing commentary, and by offering action suggestions (as in our example of Sophie nesting the Russian dolls, and also referred to by DeLoache and Brown); aiding the presentation of appropriate, comprehensible and increasingly sophisticated accounts of behaviour, which involves concepts, language content and appropriate styles of language use.

The second theme of discourse is the *co-construction of meaning*. This is truly a bridge between the individual and social orientations. Meaning is created through co-construction in dyads and groups, but the child does not merely absorb the public concept; she must reformulate it herself in order to internalize it.

Judy Dunn cites interactions between parent and child, and between siblings, where there is a negotiation of meaning going on. In some cases the mother is first explicating and then confirming the child's observations. In other cases mother and child are working towards an agreed definition of what is happening, or what the child is feeling. In the examples Helen Haste quotes, especially from the work of Damon on children's negotiation of sharing, children bring to the debate a range of possible alternative strategies and, through discussion, come to some kind of agreement. Such outcomes are not merely a consensus about one of the alternatives; the discussion itself generates a new set of criteria as well as rehearsing existing criteria.

For a theoretical analysis of the mechanisms by which *meaning is created* in discourse we must turn to the chapters by Bruner and Feldman. Bruner explores the young child's capacity to achieve a common reference with others, and how this is the basis for the process of discourse itself. The earliest manifestations of this are the child following the gaze of the mother, paying attention to what she is attending to – as we have already said, the mother's manipulation of this early form of 'discourse' is part of the scaffolding process described above. But children – and adults – have to make things unambiguous – or less ambiguous – in order to understand them, and most particularly in order to engage in effective discourse. Bruner argues that very young children are able to work out what is being referred to in an expression, and also what other expressions are implied. So in discourse, the child, even from a very early age (around 2) has the skills to infer the meanings implied by the other, and to use such inferences in interaction.

Much of Feldman's chapter is a theoretical analysis of the process of making meaning in discourse. Her 'epistemic–ontic shift', described earlier, is intra-individual, but has cultural consequences. She explains how discourse can be seen as a progression from *comments* on 'new' material (the epistemic) to *topics* – material that is now 'old' and established in the particular discourse (the ontic). The construction of a 'topic' in discourse is, she argues, the creation of a representation, which can eventually be 'dumped' in her terms and become part of the metacognition of the situation, the given, the taken-for-granted. Discourse, to be effective, requires that individuals tacitly understand the rules which differentiate comment and topic, the epistemic and the ontic. It also requires that the participants have a common store of referents, a shared 'ontic dump'. Young children do not have the ability to follow the comment–topic distinction, and it is the parent, monitoring the child's expressions of her thinking, who maintains the flow of meaning. At the start, they also show no ability to 'dump'. But as the child acquires the skills of discourse, she learns to negotiate the epistemic-ontic interrelationship.

The final theme of discourse is the way in which social representations are made evident, enacted or expressed in metaphor or in the language of legitimation. We have already noted, in Judy Dunn's work, how mothers (and siblings) draw attention to the distress of others, and suggest remedies. In Barbara Lloyd's work we have seen that mothers express overtly the defining characteristics of gender, and gender-mark certain toys and behaviour quite directly. In the various studies quoted by Helen Haste, there are many examples of a parent, peer or teacher explicity stating a rule or expectation which reflects the direct transmission of a cultural message.

But the processes of discourse are subtle, and it is not only *content* that the child must learn. She must learn *reason*. In the study of how a child comes to explain absence from school, cited earlier, the child was not only learning how to excuse absence, but that an *excuse was expected*. Style of discourse must also be mastered – when to use linguistic and when paralinguistic cues, when to take for granted; so too the *range* of discourse – that 'family' words are not universal, that 'us and them' is a primary social category. It is by such subtle means, as well as by more direct linguistic forms such as metaphors and symbols, narratives and images, that the child picks up the vast array of messages about social categories, expectations of behaviour etc., that she needs to cope with the social and conceptual world.

In conclusion, we can return to our opening comment: 'a quiet revolution has taken place in developmental psychology'. It is a revolution that reflects not only advances in empirical study but also progress in our philosophical assumptions as students of the human condition. Psychology, like many of the other human sciences, has begun to shed its heritage of nineteenth-century positivism. Its new emphasis is upon the achievement of meaning, both individually and culturally, and there is a realization now that the two are inseparable.

References

Berger, P., and Luckmann, T., *The Social Construction of Reality*. Harmondsworth: Penguin, 1966.

Breakwell, G.M., 'Women: group or identity?' *Women's Studies International Quarterly*, 1979, 2, 9–17.

Geertz, C., *The Interpretation of Cultures*. New York: Basic Books, 1973.

Hughes, M., and Donaldson, M., 'The use of hiding games for studying the co-ordination of viewpoints', *Educational Review*, 1979, 31, 133–40.

Karmiloff-Smith, A., 'Children's problem-solving', in M. Lamb, A.L. Brown and B. Rogoff (eds) *Advances in Developmental Psychology*, Volume III. Hillsdale, NJ: Erlbaum, 1987.

Moscovici, S., 'The phenomenon of social representations', in R. Farr and S. Moscovici (eds), *Social Representations*. Cambridge: Cambridge University Press, 1984.

Tajfel, H., *Human Groups and Social Categories*. Cambridge: Cambridge University Press, 1981.

Vygotsky, L., *Mind in Society*. Cambridge, Mass.: Harvard University Press, 1978.

Williams, J., and Giles, H., 'The changing status of women in society: an intergroup perspective', in H. Tajfel (ed.), *Differentiation Between Social Groups*. New York: Academic Press, 1978.

1

Understanding feelings: the early stages

JUDY DUNN

When do children begin to understand the feelings and wishes of other people in their world? It is a crucially important development for an individual born into a complex social world. Yet we know relatively little about the beginning of this understanding. Answers to the question have been sought in two ways: first, by giving children experimental tasks that require them to take perspective of another, to report on the feelings of a story-book character, or to identify an emotional state from a picture or drawing; second – and much less frequently – by attempting to make inferences about children's understanding of another person's feelings from their naturally-occurring responses to others' behaviour or actions, and from their spontaneous conversations. Both these research strategies present major problems of interpretation, and leave the answer to our question still clouded. The difficulties presented by the second strategy are obvious. It is a hazardous business attempting to establish the nature of children's understanding simply from observing their behaviour, especially as with very young children this is frequently non-verbal behaviour.

The experimental tasks of the first strategy have resulted in a range of contradictory findings, and the interpretation of these contradictions is full of pitfalls. While it is generally accepted from experimental studies that 'significant increases in understanding others' emotions and situations that elicit emotions occur between the ages of three and six' (Shantz, 1983, p. 517), the ability of 3- and 4-year-olds to identify others' emotions remains a matter of dispute, and such studies are rarely conducted with children under 3. The early stages of children's understanding of emotion remains, from studies within this experimental paradigm, unclear. It is a familiar argument that it is in interaction with other *children* that the crucial developments in social understanding take place (Hartup, 1983). What then of the period between infancy and this stage of the arguments and disputes between articulate 5- and 6-year-olds, forcing each other to face each other's feelings and point of view? The period of transition from infancy to childhood has been very much a blank page as far as children's growing understanding of emotions is concerned.

The problems of tracing the beginnings of this social intelligence are formidable. One of the difficulties is that the social world in which young children first begin to develop their understanding of others' emotions is the *family* – and it is within the family that they must be studied if we are to understand the nature of the developments that take place. We know from the illuminating work of Tizard and Hughes (1984) on 4-year-olds that if children are studied within their family world the picture that we gain of their intellectual power and curiosity is dramatically different from the picture gained from studying the same children at school, or indeed from the accepted view of 4-year-olds' cognitive ability. What then of the abilities of even younger children, thinking and talking about other people in their family world? Hood and Bloom (1979) have clearly shown, in their analysis of early expressions of causality, that in their third and fourth years children talk about *psychological* causality: well before they talk about physical causality they refer to intentions and motives. In this chapter I shall discuss different lines of evidence from observational studies of even younger children at home, that demonstrate the growing capacity of children during the second year of life to read and anticipate the emotions and intentions of others. The methodology of the studies on which I shall draw has been described in detail elsewhere (Dunn and Kendrick, 1982; Dunn and Munn, 1985). They are longitudinal studies of two-child families, with observations focused upon the children's interaction with their siblings and mothers, and their response to interaction between mother and sibling. We have examined a number of different features of their behaviour and those that I shall consider here include children's behaviour in conflict, their conversations about feelings and their participation in pretend play.

The first hints that children showed considerable grasp of their siblings' feelings and wishes came from our initial study of siblings (Dunn and Kendrick, 1982). The firstborn children in that study of forty families, who were in many cases under 3 years old, made frequent comments on the feelings and intentions of their baby siblings, and indeed 'explained' the expressive behaviour and actions of the baby to the observer. The following examples are quotations from the transcripts of the tape recordings made during the observations (see Dunn and Kendrick, 1982):

Judy B: She wants to come to you.
Bruce S: He likes that. He a silly boy.
Harvey M: He likes me.
Jim E: Jackie not like monkey. (after Jackie had thrown down toy monkey)
Laura W: Callum's laughing for his dinner isn't he? He sometimes gets Bonzo's dinner [the dog's] 'cause he likes his dinner quick.
Jill J (showing O a toy): He likes this. He likes it squeaky.
Laura W: Callum's crying 'cause he wants his food cold.
Harvey M: Ronnie's happy.

There were many incidents in which the firstborn children commented on the baby's behaviour in a way that appeared to be 'detached': it did not reflect the interests of the first child, but was finely tuned to the baby's apparent wishes. It is important to note that the firstborn were sometimes quite explicit about the baby's feelings being different from their own:

Bruce S (B playing with a balloon): He going to pop it in a minute. And he'll cry. And he'll be frightened of me too. I like the pop.

Laura W (to baby sibling): You don't remember Judy. I do.

These observations do not fit the interpretation put forward for instance by Chandler and Greenspan (1972) that children of this age can merely project their own feelings onto others. These children were not confused about the situation of self and 'other' when the 'other' was their sibling.

From these comments on the baby's feelings and capabilities, and from the children's empathetic responses to their baby siblings' distress, we concluded that children of 3 were skilful at reading, anticipating and responding to the feelings of their baby siblings. Most strikingly, a few incidents in that study suggested that the secondborn siblings – aged only 14–15 months – were beginning to grasp how to comfort and how to provoke their older siblings. In the next two studies of siblings we pursued this possibility in more detail, following second-born children through the second and third year of their lives. The fights, disputes, conversations and games of the children's family life provided a context in which different aspects of the children's growing understanding of other people were re-vealed. We first consider conflict.

Family conflict

In the course of the second year children's behaviour when involved in disputes with their siblings or parents changes markedly (see Dunn and Munn, 1985, for a detailed analysis of these changes). One development that indicates a growing grasp of the feelings of the person with whom the child is in conflict is the appearance of teasing behaviour. As young as 14 months some children, in confrontation with their siblings, perform acts that apparently reflect some understanding of what will annoy the other person. Very often, at this age, the act involves removal of the older child's comfort object or destruc-tion of his or her favourite possession. By 20–24 months however the teasing becomes more elaborate: for instance one child whose older sister had three imaginary friends named Lily, Alleluia and Peepee would in the course of disputes announce that *she* was Alleluia. It was an act that was followed by fury or distress on her sister's part, and was surprisingly

sophisticated behaviour for a 24-month-old, involving transformation of identity as well as some understanding that the act
would provoke her sister. Forty-three per cent of the 18-month-
olds were observed to tease their older siblings, and forty-eight
per cent of the 24-month-olds. They also anticipated their
mothers' response to their physical aggression and teasing acts.
There was a significant difference in the probability that they
would appeal to the mother for help after they had teased or
been physically aggressive, and the probability that they would
appeal to the mother after the *sibling* had acted in these ways.
Appeals were made by the secondborn in only 4 per cent of
incidents in which they had teased or been physically aggressive, but in 66 per cent of incidents in which the sibling had
acted in this way.

In these children's family lives there was also, of course,
plenty of opportunity to witness disputes between others, and
we examined systematically the children's responses to arguments between their siblings and their mothers. They rarely
ignored such interactions: arguments and quarrels were clearly
of much salience to them. And our analyses of their responses
showed that certain features of the dispute – such as the
emotion expressed by the antagonists – were closely linked to
the children's response. If the sibling or mother was upset or
angry, the children were more likely to watch, or to act in a
supportive manner, than to laugh, imitate or punish. They
acted, that is, in a manner appropriate to the needs of one of the
antagonists, and provided practical support. Their response to
disputes in which the sibling was amused or teasing the mother
was very different. They were most likely to join the sibling in
laughing. By 24 months the children sometimes commented
explicitly, during disputes, upon the feeling state of themselves
or others, or on the responsibility of the other people for the
dispute.

It appears from the children's behaviour in these family
conflict incidents that they do during the second year develop a
considerable pragmatic understanding of what will annoy or
distress others. They use this understanding in their relationships with mother and with sibling as a source of power, in
conflicts of interest. They also use it as a source of shared
humour with other family members. They make jokes – looking

and laughing when someone transgresses, in a manner that strongly suggests some grasp of the shared nature of the rules that have been broken, and of the expectations about family behaviour.

Conversations about feeling states: deceit and narrative

Our analyses of the conversations about feeling states between the children and their mothers and siblings showed that the children not only discussed the *cause* of feelings (Dunn, Bretherton and Munn, 1987), but also used their understanding of feeling states for an impressively wide range of social functions. They communicated about feeling states when they attempted to reassure, to comfort, to provoke, to prohibit and to restrain. Especially interesting were incidents in which children apparently attempted to deceive their mothers about feeling states in their efforts to gain what they wanted. In the following example a 24-month-old girl, very lively and definitely *not* tired, demanded chocolate cake. When her demand was refused she 'put on' a tired voice to say 'Tired', and repeated the demand:

Family T. Child 24 months. Child sees chocolate cake on table.
Child: Bibby on.
Mother: You don't want your bibby on. You're not eating.
Child: Chocolate cake. Chocolate cake.
Mother: You're not having any more chocolate cake either.
Child: Why? (whines) Tired.
Mother: You tired? Ooh!
Child: Chocolate cake.
Mother: No chance.

Children also referred to feeling states when they discussed earlier events with their mothers. In the next example the 21-month-old boy started a conversation about an argument that he and his mother had had that morning over breakfast, and reenacted his own distress:

Family Cha. Child 21 months. Child refers to breakfast-time argument with mother.
Child: Eat my Weetabix. Eat my Weetabix. Crying.

Mother: Crying weren't you? We had quite a battle. 'One more
   mouthful Michael.' And what did you do? You spat it out!
Child: ('cries').

Such examples demonstrate the very different pragmatic functions for which children refer to feeling states, and the ease with
which they do so. While the 'deceit' example is of course open
to other interpretations it appears less surprising when we
consider that children of this age very frequently 'play' with
pretend feeling states, a topic that we turn to next.

Pretend play

It is often suggested that the context of pretend play provides
children with an opportunity to explore the social roles and
rules of their world (see for instance Bretherton, 1984). During
the unstructured observations of our studies many of the
children engaged in fantasy play, both alone and with their
mothers and siblings, and our analyses of this play showed not
only that they did explore social roles and rules as early as 24
months, but also that they 'played' with feeling states. A very
high proportion of their conversations with the sibling about
feeling states – 94 per cent – took place within a framework of
pretend play. The themes of these sequences of imaginative
play which the siblings set up together frequently involved
discussion and negotiation about pain, distress, sleepiness,
hunger or sadness (see Dunn, Bretherton and Munn, 1987, for a
detailed report). This discussion of feeling states within a
pretend framework is striking for two reasons. First it shows us
how salient and interesting the topic of feeling states and
emotions is for young children – it is so often what they choose
to 'play' with. Second it demonstrates their ability to 'take on' a
feeling state other than their own, to assign a pretend state to a
pretend character, and to *share* this assignment of pretend
feeling states with another. Within these pretend games the
children did not simply obey the directions of their older
siblings – 'You're tired now, go to sleep', but they offered
suggestions and made innovatory contributions in the course of
the fantasy. This is remarkably mature behaviour for children of
only 24 months. Particularly striking was the finding that even

at 18 months some children were able in the context of pretend play with an affectionate and supportive older sibling to take part in a shared fantasy involving feeling states other than their own.

Such games occurred in a minority of families. In two separate studies we found that between a quarter and a third of the sibling pairs played in this way. It was in those families in which the sibling relationship was particularly warm and friendly that such games occurred (Dunn and Dale, 1984). To set up and maintain such play, affectionate interest of both children in each other appears to be essential. The experience of such play may in itself contribute to the affectionate quality of the relationship. If the children's experiences in these joint pretend games are indeed as important in the development of social understanding as psychologists have suggested (Bretherton, 1984), then it seems we should take seriously the potential importance of individual differences in sibling relationships.

Stories and television

The interest that 2-year-old children showed in other people was evident not only in their pretend play but in conversations that the children had with their mothers and siblings over stories, and while watching television. Here, for instance, is a 2-year-old from our first study looking at a book with her mother:

Virginia L and Mother.
Child: Great big bonfire.
Mother: Big bonfire, yes, it is a great big bonfire. What is it burning up the bonfire?
Child: Burning birdies. All hungry.
Mother: They've got to fly away because they've burned the tree that the birdies used to live in, haven't they? And look at all the little bunny rabbits crying.
Child: They sad.
Mother: That's right, they're sad.

Our findings here parallel those of Tizard and Hughes in their study of 4-year-olds. Book reading was often resorted to by mothers when their children were fractious and tired, and was not usually the idyllic moment of rapport between mother and child that's often portrayed in literature about parenting. However children were, as in the examples given by Tizard and Hughes, often clearly upset by incidents or pictures in books and sought reassurance from their mothers, and in doing so both explored the emotional situation of the story-book character and 'explained' the reasons for their distress. The child in the next example (Dunn, Bretherton and Munn, 1987) was only 24-months-old, yet in her conversation manages to make the cause of her distress clear.

Family Th. Child 24 months. Older sibling has been showing child a book with pictures of monsters. Child leaves sibling and goes to mother.
Child: Mummy. Mummy (whines).
Mother: What's wrong?
Child: Frighten.
Mother: The book?
Child: Yes.
Mother: It's not frightening you!
Child: Yes!
Mother: It did, did it?
Child: Yes.

The distress of others

The early development of empathetic responses to other people's distress remains a topic on which there is still little systematic data, in spite of the role it has been assigned in various theoretical discussions of the development of altruistic behaviour, and in moral development. The important study by Zahn-Waxler and Yarrow still stands very much alone (Cummings, Zahn-Waxler and Yarrow, 1981; Yarrow and Waxler, 1975).

Our infant subjects supplied very provocative data on sensitivity to affective states of others. Responses were by no means universal. However very young children were often finely discriminative and responsive to others' need states. Children in the youngest cohort showed distress to parental arguments and anger with each other. Responses were sometimes marked: crying, holding hands over ears, comforting a distraught parent, or (punitively) hitting the parent perceived as the guilty one. Parental affection toward each other was equally arousing: children of 1 to 2 and a half tried to join in or to separate the parents – even kicking the mother's leg. One child, from 15 months to 2 years, showed consistently different responses depending on whether mother or father initiated the affectionate hug or kiss. Initiation by the mother aroused no affect in the child, whereas with the father's (or grandfather's) initiation toward the mother, the child would 'fall apart' (hitting, glaring, sucking her thumb).

Around one year most of the youngest cohort first showed comfort to a person crying or in pain by patting, hugging or presenting an object. Among 1 and a half and 2 year olds comforting was sometimes sophisticated and elaborate, e.g. fixing the hurt by trying to put a Band-aid on, covering mother with a blanket when she was resting, trying to locate the source of the difficulty. Children also began to express concern verbally, and sometimes gave suggestions about how to deal with the problem. Such precocity on the part of the very young gives one pause. The capabilities for compassion, for various kinds of reaching out to others in a giving sense are viable and effective responses early in life. (Yarrow and Waxler, 1975, pp. 78–9)

In our own studies of two-child families, the 18- and 24-month-old children's responses to the distress of their siblings relatively rarely included attempts to *comfort* them. This is perhaps not surprising, since the children were usually the *cause* of the siblings' distress. As we have already noted, the children knew well how to upset their siblings, and often responded to their distress by exacerbating the situation. The failure to comfort was not, it appears, because they did not understand the emotional state of the sibling but, rather, reflected the children's motivation – to upset and not to comfort the competitor. The topic of distress was one of the most common themes of the conversations about feeling states, and mothers frequently articulated the cause of the distress. Children as young as 24 months themselves often pointed out the cause of others' distress, as the next example illustrates:

Family M. Child 24 months. Baby sibling is crying after child
   knocked him (accidentally). Mother comes into room.
Child: Poor Thomas.
Mother: What?
Child: I banged his head.
Mother: You banged it?
Child: Yes.
Mother: Are you going to kiss it?
Child: Yes.
Mother: Kiss his head.

It was in such discussions that individual differences between
families were particularly striking. In some families mothers'
conversational turns concerning feeling states occurred as often
as ten per hour, in other families they were much more rare.
Now Zahn-Waxler and Yarrow reported that in families in
which mothers drew their children's attention clearly, consistently and insistently to distress of others that the children had
caused, the children were at a later time point more concerned
and altruistic towards others than children whose mothers did
not discuss the cause of distress in this fashion. Zahn-Waxler
and Yarrow's data was based on mothers' reports of their
children's behaviour. How do our direct observations fit with
their findings – and how significant in the development of
children's understanding are such differences in maternal
discussion of feelings?

Individual differences

Not only were there marked differences between the mothers in
the frequency of their comments about feeling states to the
children, but these differences were stable over time (Dunn,
Bretherton and Munn, 1987). The correlation between the
proportion of maternal utterances concerned with feeling states
at 18 and at 24 months was for instance $r(42)=0.63$. It is
interesting to note that Beeghly and Mervis (1984) in a
longitudinal study of mothers' speech to 13-, 20- and 28-month-
olds which examined the mothers' speech in three different
contexts (free play, snack time and story reading) found that

individual differences in mothers' references to internal states were stable across contexts and across age periods – the only variable that they measured that was stable in this way.

In our study these differences between mothers in their discussion of feeling states were correlated over time with differences between *children* in the proportion of their conversation that concerned feeling states. For instance, the proportion of maternal conversational turns about feelings at 18 months was correlated r(42)=0.62 with the proportion of children's conversational turns that concerned feeling states at 24 months. There was a similar pattern of correlations between the siblings' conversational turns about feeling states at 18 months and the children's conversational turns at 24 months.

The analysis also showed marked and consistent differences in the frequency of such conversations in families with girls and with boys. Mothers talked more to 18-month-old daughters about feelings than they did to 18-month-old sons. By 24 months the daughters themselves talked more about feeling states than did the sons. With a sample of only forty-three families such gender differences must of course be regarded with caution, however with the recent evidence for differences between women and men in the way in which they reflect on feelings in relation to moral issues (Gilligan, 1982) the findings do take on some importance.

It is of course likely that differences between mothers in their discussion of feeling states with their very young children are linked to other differences in their relationship with their children, and any or all of these differences in maternal behaviour may be important in contributing to the later differences in the children. In our first sibling study (Dunn and Kendrick, 1982) we found a network of correlations between the frequency of mothers' references to the needs, wants and feelings of the newborn sibling, their references to the motives and intentions of others, their use of language for complex cognitive purposes and their use of justification for control. Mothers who talked to their 2-year-olds with a high frequency of these references were most likely to encourage their firstborn to discuss how the new baby should be cared for, and to take part in this caregiving. They were also more likely to enter the child's world of pretend by making pretend suggestions and comments than other mothers. One year after the sibling was born, the children from these families in which the mothers had talked to them about the feelings of the new baby were more friendly to the sibling than the children from families in which the mothers had not talked to them in this way – and, most strikingly, the babies themselves were also more friendly to their older siblings. However the network of correlations between the different aspects of mothers' talk and behaviour means that we should not assume a simple causal link between one particular feature of the mothers' conversation – such as reference to the feeling states of others – and the children's later behaviour. The differences in how mothers talk appear, rather, to reflect a particular style of relating to a 2-year-old. Yet the results do suggest that in families in which mother and child engage in such conversations, the children are likely to become particularly articulate about and interested in feeling states. We should not ignore the potential developmental importance of such discussions.

Children's interest in other people

The behaviour of these very young children in their fights, play and conversations suggests that within the family context children are beginning to show much more advanced social understanding than we would have expected on the basis of their performance in more formal experimental tasks. As 2-year-olds their essays into discussion of motives and feelings – both their own and those of other people – have hardly begun, but the interest and attention they show in why and how people behave in the way that they do is already evident. As Tizard and Hughes (1984) show it is an interest that blossoms in the family world, so that by four years old:

> Interest in other people – both children and adults – was a characteristic feature of most of the children in the study and manifested itself in many different topics: their friends, other members of the family, growing up, birth, illness and death, what people did for their living and so on. Indeed, it is worth remarking on the breadth of the children's interests, and the complexity of the issues which they raised. It is sometimes

supposed that children of this age have special, childish interests, mainly to do with mothers, babies, dolls, teddies and animals, and such a view would be reinforced by most of the picture books published for children of this age. The conversations in our study suggest that, on the contrary, all human experience was grist to their intellectual mill. (Tizard and Hughes, 1984, p. 128)

Even as 2-year-olds the children in our studies were beginning to take part in such conversations, and it seems very plausible that the discussion of cause and consequence of feelings in the emotional context of family disputes and games and the experience of *playing* at others' emotions in shared games with the sibling do contribute to the development of this intelligent concern with others. Other features of family life are surely important too: the familiarity and intimacy of family members, the shared life-world of the siblings, the emotional intensity of the relationships, the uninhibited expression of this emotion and the continuing stream of explanations by mothers of why people feel and behave the way that they do. Within these English families children (girls especially) are exposed to and expected to take part in conversations and discussions about feeling states from early in the second year. To understand more clearly the ways in which the emotional quality of family relationships, a mother's close attunement to her child's interests, the relationship with the sibling and the particular context of conversation each affect these early stages of the development of social intelligence it is family interaction that must be studied. At present we can only guess at the part these different factors play. But it is already clear that unless we study these very young children within their family world we run the risk of gravely misrepresenting their interest in and abilities to understand feelings – their own and those of other people. As Tizard and Hughes show so clearly for 4-year-olds, it is the social world, and the feeling states of others as a particular theme running through that world, that are of absorbing interest to these 2-year-olds.

40 *Making Sense*

References

Beeghly, M., and Mervis, C.B., 'Mothers' internal state labelling to toddlers'. Paper presented at the Fourth International Conference on Infant Studies, New York, April 1984.

Bretherton, I. (ed.), *Symbolic Play: The Development of Social Understanding*. New York: Academic Press, 1984.

Chandler, M.J., and Greenspan, S., 'Ersatz egocentrism: a reply to H. Borke', *Developmental Psychology*, 1972, 7, 104–6.

Cummings, E.M., Zahn-Waxler, C., and Yarrow, M.R., 'Young children's response to expression of anger and affection by others in the family', *Child Development*, 1981, 52, 1274–82.

Donaldson, M., *Children's Minds*. London: Collins, 1978.

Dunn, J., Bretherton, I., and Munn, P., 'Conversations about feeling states between mothers and their young children', *Developmental Psychology*, 1987, 23, 1–8.

Dunn, J., and Dale, N., 'I a Daddy: 2-year-olds' collaboration in joint pretend with sibling and with mother', in I. Bretherton (ed.), *Symbolic Play: The Development of Social Understanding*. New York: Academic Press, 1984.

Dunn, J., and Kendrick, C., *Siblings: Love, Envy and Understanding*. Cambridge, Mass.: Harvard University Press, 1982.

Dunn, J., and Munn, P., 'Becoming a family member: family conflict and the development of social understanding in the second year', *Child Development*, 1985, 56, 480–92.

Gilligan, C., *In a Different Voice*. Cambridge, Mass.: Harvard University Press, 1982.

Hartup, W.W., 'Peer relations', in P. Mussen (ed.), *Handbook of Child Psychology*, Volume IV: *Socialisation, Personality and Social Development*. New York: Wiley, 1983.

Hood, L., and Bloom, L., *What, When and How About Why: A Longitudinal Study of Expressions of Causality*. Monographs of the Society for Research in Child Development, No. 181, vol. 44, no. 6.

Shantz, C.U., 'Social cognition', in J.H. Flavell and E.M. Markman (eds), *Handbook of Child Psychology*, Volume III: *Cognitive Development*. New York: Wiley, 1983.

Tizard, B., and Hughes, M., *Young Children Learning*. London: Fontana, 1984.

Yarrow, M.R., and Waxler, C.Z., 'The emergence and functions of prosocial behaviour in young children'. Paper presented at the Society for Research in Child Development meeting, Denver, 1975.

2
Taking roles
PAUL LIGHT

This chapter is about role-taking, a concept which has assumed a high profile in developmental psychology in the last ten or fifteen years. I shall review the background of this research 'boom' briefly, and then go on to appraise some of the methods which have been used to study role-taking development. In the latter part of the chapter I shall focus on the relationship between role-taking and social behaviour, where an alternative to the currently prevailing 'cognitive developmental' viewpoint seems to be emerging.

Introduction: egocentrism and social role-taking

As a topic for detailed developmental research, role-taking dates back only to the late 1960s. However, as a developmental construct its origins go back considerably further, and most clearly to the early writings of Piaget and G.H. Mead. It may be useful at the outset to offer a very brief outline of these early standpoints.

The key Piagetian concept is that of egocentrism. Piaget used the concept of egocentrism to draw together individual and social aspects of thinking. Thus the child was held to 'centre' on one aspect of an object or situation to the neglect of other relevant aspects, so that his reasoning was distorted. Similarly he was held to 'centre' on his own viewpoint in a social situation, making effective communication and cooperation impossible. In the social domain development consists in a shift from this egocentric state towards one in which the child can move flexibly and reversibly from one perspective to another, achieving social reciprocity. In the strictly intellectual domain a similar transition is reflected in the achievement of concrete operational thinking: the child's thought shows increasing flexibility and reversibility, allowing him to establish relations and classes which are decentralized with respect to himself.

In his earlier writings Piaget (e.g. 1932, 1950) took the view that interindividual reciprocity was established through social experience, with intellectual decentration following from this social decentration. However he later withdrew somewhat from this position (e.g. Piaget and Inhelder, 1969), continuing to emphasize the parallel between intellectual and social decentration, but assigning causal priority to neither. By contrast, G.H. Mead was irrevocably committed to the claim that experience gained through social interaction provided the foundation for individual intellectual development.

The same phenomena which Piaget described in terms of the diminution of egocentrism, Mead (1934) described in terms of emerging self-awareness. He argued that self-awareness is only attained by an individual indirectly, through social activity. In social exchanges the child brings himself into his own field of experience as a social object, by taking the role of others towards himself. Role-taking, in Mead's sense, refers to the cognitive process of 'putting oneself in the place of' another person and making inferences concerning the other's experiences. In particular it involves conceptualizing one's own interaction with the other as seen through the other's eyes.

The implications of role-taking were seen to extend beyond social behaviour to encompass all aspects of mental development. At the outset, the child does not distinguish between his awareness of, or perspective on, a situation and that situation itself. In the process of development the child is gradually made aware of the fact that a situation in which he and others are engaged may look very different from different perspectives. The development of role-taking (i.e. the awareness of a diversity of possible perspectives) permits the child a degree of detachment from his own perspective, this detachment being a necessary condition for objectivity of thought in all domains.

Mead's theory thus shared with Piaget's the characterization of the young child's thought as inflexible and 'centred', and both theorists emphasized the close ties between developments in the social sphere and those in the realm of 'impersonal' cognition. 'Egocentrism' is in many respects simply the converse of 'role-taking', a point made explicit by Flavell who, in a book which did much to open up this field to detailed research, stated that 'intellectual egocentrism is fundamentally an inability to take roles' (1968, p. 17). Flavell's preference for the term 'role-taking' reflected merely the choice of the positive as opposed to the negative pole. Other developmental researchers have preferred the term 'perspective taking'; in practice these terms can be regarded as synonymous.

Mead's and Piaget's theories have thus largely converged, and Flavell's research initiative set the tone for a theoretically eclectic approach drawing on both theories. Later in this chapter I shall have occasion to return to some of the issues which differentiate them. At this point, though, a thumbnail sketch is needed of the proliferation of empirical research on role-taking since 1968. In the sections which follow I shall try to give some indication of the wide variety of approaches which have been adopted to the assessment of role-taking abilities in childhood. Many of the most influential studies have been concerned with seeing another's point of view in the most literal sense, being concerned with the child's ability to infer the content of another's field of vision. Work in this area will be considered first.

Visual perspective-taking

Piaget and Inhelder's 'three-mountain' study has become a key reference point for research on visuo-spatial egocentrism. Children were presented with a three-dimensional model of three mountains and were asked to identify the perspective of a doll which occupied viewing positions different from their own. Results obtained with this task led Piaget and Inhelder to say of the typical 4- and 5-year-old that he 'appears to be rooted in his own viewpoint in the narrowest and most restrictive fashion so that he cannot imagine any perspective but his own' (1956, p. 242).

Piaget and Inhelder were in fact referring to a study (or rather a series of studies) first reported in the 1930s by Edith Meyer (Morss, 1983), and the extent to which the younger children really did attribute their *own* view to the doll is not entirely clear from either account. Moreover, in the same volume Piaget and Inhelder (1956) report studies in which children were asked to represent, by drawing, other people's views of single, relatively simple objects. As with the three-mountains task the youngest children were apparently unable to take account of the viewer's position, but their drawings did not reflect their own view of the objects. Instead they showed a 'canonical' view: one showing the object to its best advantage. Recent research offers findings consistent with this. The reason why young children frequently disregard viewpoint in their drawings continues to exercise researchers (e.g. Freeman and Cox, 1985; Light and Simmons, 1983) but it is quite clear that in this context they disregard not only the other's viewpoint but also their own. In fact, within the format of perspective-taking tasks young children are often unable to answer questions about their *own* view, and because of artefacts in such tasks what appears as an 'own view' bias in children's selections of pictures may often in reality be a *best view* bias (Liben and Belknap, 1981; Light and Nix, 1983).

It seems, then, that the child's supposed preoccupation with his own view may be more apparent than real. Where others have found such 'egocentric' response tendencies in perspective-taking tasks these have frequently been explicable as misunderstandings about the task or as 'fall-back' responses in the face of information overload. Piaget and Inhelder's conclusion, quoted earlier, that the young child is 'locked into' his own visual experience appears to be an inappropriate one.

Piaget himself has elsewhere characterized egocentrism not so much as a fixation on one point of view but rather as a *failure to differentiate between points of view* (e.g. Piaget, 1962), and this position certainly accords more happily with the available evidence. However, while 4- and 5-year-olds may certainly fail to differentiate points of view on occasions, and may be unable to construe another's viewpoint under some circumstances, recent research has clearly shown that such incapacity is far from total. For example, on tasks requiring the child to choose a picture showing another observer's view, even 3½-year-olds can do well if only a single object such as toy fire engine is used (Fishbein, Lewis and Keiffer, 1972). Even multiple-object arrays can be handled at this age if they consist of very familiar 'fronted' objects such as model farm animals (Borke, 1975). Moreover 3- and 4-year-olds can successfully *hide* a doll from one or more others (Hughes and Donaldson, 1979; Light, 1979) and children from 2 onwards will usually turn a picture towards another person to show it to him (Lempers, Flavell and Flavell, 1977). Pointing and gaze-following offer even earlier indications of a recognition that the other's visual experience is not necessarily the same as the child's own. Chapter 3, by Butterworth, offers a review of the relevant infancy literature.

It is clear, then, that we cannot properly regard the preschool child, or even the infant, as wholly ignorant of others' visual experience. But it is equally clear that the various tasks and measures used are measuring very different things. The best sustained attempt to lend order to research in this area is Flavell's 'developmental model'. This identifies four levels which, he suggests, 'may well constitute a regular, possibly invariant, developmental sequence of cognitive acquisitions' (1974, p. 100). The most significant distinction for present purposes is between levels one and two. The level-one child is supposed to be able to make inferences about *what* another person can or can't see from a given position. Only at level two, however, is the child supposed to understand the idea of people having different perspectives or views of the same display. The 'three-mountains' task clearly makes level-two demands. In a study exemplifying level-one demands, 3-year-olds were asked to say whether the experimenter saw a cat or a dog when a card with a drawing of a cat on one side and a dog on the other was held vertically between experimenter and child. All the children tested could answer this type of question without difficulty (Flavell *et al.*, 1981).

The level-one/level-two distinction is an important one, and needs to be kept in mind in any comparison of the results of different tasks. For example a task in which a doll hides from one or more policemen has been found to be a great deal easier than the 'three-mountains' task. Hughes and Donaldson suggest that this is because the policemen tasks make *human sense* in a way that the mountain task does not (1983, p. 253). But clearly in Flavell's terms the policeman tasks are level-one tasks, requiring inferences only about what the policeman can and cannot see, whereas the mountains task is a level-two task.

There is, however, little reason for supposing that these 'levels' reflect developmental stages in any neat and tidy sense. Within any level, tasks can be of very variable difficulty levels. Moreover in practice it may be difficult to categorize tasks as belonging to this or that level. For example, in Fishbein, Lewis and Keiffer's study, mentioned earlier, the child may correctly judge that the observer opposite him will see 'the back of the fire engine'. Is this a *view* of an object in a common visual space (level two), or an *aspect* of the object visible only to the other (level one)? So even within the domain of visual perspective-taking, to which it is restricted, this attempt at systematization is not without its problems.

In the section which follows I shall broaden the field of research under consideration by turning from measures of visual perspective-taking to measures of children's awareness of other people's thoughts and feelings.

Cognitive, affective and communicative role-taking

Role-taking involves taking account of the other's viewpoint in situations in which it differs from one's own. 'Viewpoint' in this context may refer not only to what the other person *sees*, but to what he or she knows, thinks, feels, wants, and so on. Considerable effort has been put into devising procedures for measuring children's abilities in this respect. The briefest of reviews will set the scene.

Social guessing games provide one entrée. In guessing which of two hands a penny is held in, is the child considering which way the other person will be *expecting* him to guess (De Vries, 1970)? At what age can the child understand the 'thought bubble' convention of the comic strip (Miller, Kessel and Flavell, 1970)? Using approaches such as these it has been shown that from 6 or 7 years of age children can make judgements regarding others' expectations and can begin to see that their own thoughts can be included as objects of the other's thinking.

A number of assessment methods rather more explicitly require the child to make inferences about what another person does or doesn't know. For example, the child might see and hear a videotaped story and then see his mother watch the video with the sound turned down. Under these circumstances 4- and 5-year-olds turn out to be fairly successful at judging what their mothers would and wouldn't know about the story (Mossler, Marvin and Greenberg, 1976). A related procedure involves having the child tell a story involving a number of characters from a cartoon strip, and then having him retell the story from the point of view of one of the characters in the story (e.g. Chandler, Greenspan and Barenboim, 1974). The stories are designed so that certain privileged information is available to the child as reader but not to the character whose perspective he has to adopt. Children under about 7 typically fail to make the required differentiation.

A somewhat more clinical, less experimental, approach has been adopted by Selman (1980; Selman, Lavin and Brion-Meisels, 1982) who has constructed a series of 'sociomoral dilemmas'. These are stories involving more or less complex or ambiguous motives, emotional reactions, etc., about which children of different ages are extensively interviewed. The technique has much in common with that of Kohlberg (e.g. 1976) in the field of moral judgement, and, like Kohlberg, Selman has elaborated a structural developmental model involving various stages and levels of social perspective-taking. Lying, and deception generally, clearly depends upon specific attributions of knowledge and ignorance to others, and the development of deliberate deception would seem to be a promising avenue of approach to cognitive role-taking. It has received little attention until recently but it would appear that 4- and 5-year-olds are beginning to sort out some of the distinctions involved (e.g. Perner, Gruber and Wimmer, 1985). Certainly everyday experience suggests that deceit becomes much more prevalent (and successful) from about this age.

One of the more contentious areas of role-taking research has concerned children's ability to make judgements about the emotional responses of others. Borke (1973) devised a non-verbal assessment procedure which involved presenting pre-schoolers with a series of short stories relating to a character who was represented by a blank faced picture. The children were asked to indicate how this character would be feeling by selecting an appropriate emotional expression and placing it in the picture. Children as young as 3 performed quite well on this task. However, as Chandler (1977) has pointed out, children may well be responding simply on the basis of associative connections between particular situations (e.g. having a birthday) and particular emotions (e.g. being happy). Ideally one would like to put the child's own perspective in conflict with that of the target character, but in the case of affective role-taking this raises obvious difficulties.

Piaget originally introduced the concept of egocentrism in relation to failure of verbal communication (Piaget, 1926). To communicate effectively, he argued, the speaker must take account of his listener in shaping his utterance. This has formed the basis for a further line of role-taking research, must of it using a paradigm established by Krauss and Glucksberg (1969). For example, two children might be seated on opposite sides of a screen, each having in front of him a standard set of pictures. One child (the speaker) must verbally specify one particular picture so that the other child (the listener) can correctly select it. Children under about 6 generally perform very poorly on such tasks, and they do not improve much with practice. When failures of communication occur, they are typically attributed to the listener who 'picked the wrong card' rather than to the speaker's inadequate message (Robinson and Robinson, 1980).

There is no doubt that preschool children can to *some* extent adjust their utterances to match their listener's requirements. For example, Maratsos (1973) asked children to tell a blindfolded, as against a sighted, listener how to play a game. He was able to show that children as young as 3 and 4 often make listener-appropriate adjustments. It is equally clear, though, that even considerably older children (or adults, for that matter) do not *always* do so. Such errors seem to reflect not so much a role-taking incapacity as a momentary lapse – a failure to *attend* adequately to the listener.

This highlights a problem common to most of the 'role-taking measures' touched upon here. When a child fails in such a task, it is sometimes difficult to decide whether the failure is, in fact, a failure of role-taking at all, as opposed to a failure in respect of some irrelevant aspect of the task. Even if it is a role-taking failure, it may still be unclear whether the child does not *know* that others have differing viewpoints, or whether he fails to appreciate that this is a task which requires such knowledge. A marked disparity between the apparent availability of role-taking inferences and the use actually made of them has often been noted.

Even more than was the case with visual perspective-taking, the measures used to assess cognitive, affective and communicative role-taking are immensely various. Attempts have been made to identify stages of development more clearly by separating tasks according to whether perspectives need to be handled successively or simultaneously or according to the degree of recursiveness of inference involved.

However, in a recent review Higgins (1981) has highlighted the fact that the tasks used may vary in the type of reasoning required to infer the other's viewpoint, and/or in the complexity of the information to be handled, and/or in the extent to which the subject's own perspective differs from that of the 'target'. He suggests that most 'stage' accounts can actually be reduced to a matter of complexity, while some, like Selman's mentioned earlier, confuse different dimensions of difference at each stage. It is notable that Higgins' characterization of what is involved in role-taking lacks the stage-like character which is so much a feature of cognitive-developmental approaches, and could be applied with equal appropriateness at any point in the lifespan.

In the absence of a well articulated and widely accepted conceptualization of the nature of the behaviour indexed by role-taking tasks, the more empirical approach of examining inter-task correlations has been adopted. The outcome of this will be considered in the following section, within the context of an examination of the relationship between role-taking development and social adjustment.

Role-taking and social adjustment

When faced with a very mixed bag of tasks all of which purport to be measuring the same underlying construct, an obvious strategy is to examine the consistency of individual performance across a range of such tasks. While age differences have been the main concern of the devisors of role-taking tasks, marked individual differences within the age groups have also been reported (e.g. Hughes, 1975; Light, 1979). Clearly, if role-taking can properly be considered as a general skill or disposition, and if available tasks offer valid and reliable measures of it, then individual differences should be reasonably stable across a range of such tasks. In this section I shall examine some of the evidence relating to the validity of the role-taking construct in this internal sense, and then go on to consider its external validity in terms of relationships with independent indices of social behaviour.

A number of studies have demonstrated significant positive intercorrelations between diverse role-taking tasks, including for example measures of visual perspective-taking, recursive thinking, referential communication and picture-story tasks (Rubin, 1973; Hollos, 1975; Light, 1979; Van Lieshout, Leckie and Smits-Van Sonsbeek, 1976). My own findings are fairly typical of this group. Eight role-taking measures were administered to a sample of sixty 4-year-olds. Virtually all intercorrelations were positive and significant, and most remained so when IQ was partialled out.

However, even in this group of studies the inter-test correlations are typically modest (averaging about 0.4 in my own study) and thus account for a rather small proportion of the variance. Moreover, a number of other studies have found little or no evidence for a unitary role-taking factor underlying all tasks. Several studies have found that correlational analysis of a battery of role-taking tasks suggests that such tasks fall into distinct groups, relatively independent of one another (e.g. Urberg and Docherty, 1976; O'Connor, 1977; O'Reilly Landry and Lyons Ruth, 1980), but the groupings are not consistent across studies. Measures of affective role-taking have sometimes been found to be independent of other types, but with some degree of consistency existing between visual perspective-taking, cognitive role-taking and referential communications measures (Ford, 1979; Krebs and Russell, 1980). In other cases complex age- and sex-dependent relationships or generally low intercorrelations have been found (e.g. Kurdek, 1977).

Some authors, not unnaturally, have used these low or variable patterns of intercorrelation to argue against the utility of role-taking as a general construct (e.g. Kurdek, 1977; Ford, 1979). Others have pointed to the questionable validity and reliability of the particular tasks used, or to their limited scoring ranges and variable difficulty levels (e.g. Hudson, 1978; Rubin, 1978; Krebs and Russell, 1980). It is true, of course, that there are countless methodological pitfalls capable of reducing levels of correlation, but it would seem that one is forced into an uncomfortable choice between questioning the role-taking construct or questioning the adequacy of the tasks available to measure it.

Many researchers have directed their efforts towards examining not the relationships of one role-taking measure to another but the relationships between role-taking and social behaviour. As was indicated earlier, both Piaget and Mead envisaged the development of role-taking as intimately connected with the development of adjusted social behaviour. Within the more recent cognitive developmental tradition role-taking has been seen as a cognitive precondition for many types of social behaviour, particularly for what has come to be known as 'prosocial behaviour'.

In 1977 Mussen and Eisenberg-Berg concluded that 'All the evidence we have reviewed leads us to conclude that, as hypothesised, role-taking ability is a forceful antecedent of prosocial behaviour' (p. 134). This conclusion seems distinctly optimistic given the problematic nature of the available evidence, then and now. Significant positive relationships have been shown between role-taking measures and measures of leadership, gregariousness, friendship and cooperation in school-aged children, though not in preschoolers (Rothenberg, 1970; Jennings, 1975; Johnson, 1975). In my own work with 4-year-olds, using a battery of role-taking tasks and maternal interview data, children who scored well on role-taking tended to be judged more socially confident and competent in a number of ways, though some rather paradoxical findings also emerged (Light, 1979). A range of role-taking measures was also used by Zahn-Waxler, Radke-Yarrow and Brady-Smith (1977) with 3- to 7-year-olds, but they did not find scores to be predictive of 'prosocial interventions' (comforting, helping and sharing).

The measures of prosocial behaviour used by Zahn-Waxler *et al.* involved the children comforting, helping or sharing with an adult. The appropriateness of this has been questioned and in another study where altruistic behaviours were observed in the context of child–child interactions, significant relationships with perceptual and affective role-taking measures *were* found (Buckley, Siegel and Ness, 1979). The issue of the adequacy of measures of prosocial behaviour is in fact a very vexed one. Almost all of the studies mentioned have relied upon contrived situations to elicit measures of prosocial behaviour. Unfortunately, it appears that children's prosocial conduct is often inconsistent across situations, and observed conduct may correlate poorly with ratings (e.g. Payne, 1980).

Moreover, the use of contrived measures may generate spurious correlations. For example, in a study which examined the prosocial behaviour of 4- and 5-year-olds in relation to an affective role-taking task, it was found that the role-taking measures correlated positively to prosocial behaviour elicited in response to a request but actually negatively to observed prosocial behaviour. The authors discuss the possibility that both contrived measures are in fact indexing the extent to which the child attempts to please the experimenter (Eisenberg-Berg and Lennon, 1980).

Thus the problems of establishing convincing relationships between role-taking and prosocial behaviour are considerable, not least because of the difficulty of defining and measuring the latter. This difficulty is perhaps less acute when one is dealing with children who manifest severe social maladjustment. Here the hypothesis is essentially that some or all of the adjustment problems encountered by these children arise from deficiencies in role-taking or related cognitive skills. Evidence has been obtained for the existence of such deficits in emotionally disturbed and aggressive children (Chandler, Greenspan and Barenboim, 1974) and in chronically delinquent boys (Chandler, 1973). In these studies attempts were made to train the children in role-taking, and improvements were claimed in the children's social behaviour. This work converges with that of Spivack and Shure on social adjustment, where role-taking is seen as a prerequisite of 'interpersonal problem-solving' (Marsh, Serafica and Barenboim, 1980; Shure, 1982).

In sum, then, the mass of largely correlational research reviewed in this section has provided evidence, albeit limited and qualified, for a positive association between role-taking measures and indices of children's social competence. The hypothesis which has motivated much of this work, namely that role-taking represents the key cognitive development underlying the growth of social competence, is thus not without support. But the serious question marks raised about the construct validity of role-taking and about the adequacy of the various indices of social behaviour cast a considerable shadow, and it cannot be claimed that this approach has yet contributed much to our detailed understanding of the development of prosocial behaviour. In the final section of this chapter I shall take a broader look at the issues raised thus far, suggesting rather different conceptualizations of the relationships involved.

On the role of role-taking in social development

We found our starting point for this consideration of research on role-taking with Piaget and Inhelder's 'three-mountains' study. This study influenced subsequent role-taking research in a number of ways. It generated much interest in visual perspective-taking, of course. More importantly, perhaps, it set the mark of Piagetian constructivism on this field of research, and much subsequent work has been primarily concerned with establishing the presence or absence of distinct competences at particular stages of development.

As we have seen, there have been a number of attempts to identify invariant sequences of role-taking development (e.g. Flavell, 1974; Selman, 1980) as well as various attempts to construct hierarchies of tasks in terms of their cognitive demands. However, this approach has met with only limited success. The empirical support for existing hierarchies of role-taking is based almost exclusively on their originators' own tests (Krebs and Russell, 1980). Fifteen years of vigorous research has not produced any stage model which can convincingly encompass more than a very limited part of the role-taking spectrum.

It is clear that early and middle childhood are periods of rapid role-taking development, but it is not clear how these age changes are best conceptualized. While most researchers have tried to characterize children's responses to role-taking tasks in terms of the presence or absence of discrete forms of psychological competence, in practice a major determinant may be the child's sensitivity to the *need* to take account of another's perspective. The effectiveness of prompting and the high degree of task-specificity of results seem to militate in favour of this kind of analysis.

While in most cases the basis of success on a task is fairly clear, the basis of failure is often not. A competence known to be available early in development may still not be reflected in performance years later. For example, a 2-year-old may sometimes turn a book for his mother to see the right way up, while a 4-year-old may sometimes fail to do so. The 6-year-old who asks 'What's this?' when his mother cannot see what he's holding presumably does not actually believe that his mother *can* see, or that she can understand his question without seeing. It seems more plausible that the child is simply, and probably temporarily, failing to attend to his listener's needs. Even adults are guilty of such lapses, of course – as Donaldson remarks 'We cannot stop to reflect on every word we utter as we hurry through a day' (1978, p. 17). There seems in fact to be a good case for supposing that role-taking performance has only a rather loose coupling to an underlying inferential competence. Thus to the extent that stable individual differences exist across a range of role-taking tasks, they might best be seen as reflecting differences in attention or sensitivity to other people's points of view rather than differences in any discrete abilities.

The influence of the cognitive-developmental approach is perhaps at its clearest in research on the relationship between role-taking and social behaviour. The envisaged scenario is roughly as follows. The young child is egocentric in the sense that his actions and perceptions are rooted in his own perspective. Gradually he learns that others have points of view separate from and potentially different from his own. He develops cognitive skills which enable him to infer the content of others' perspectives in progressively more subtle respects. As a result of these cognitive advances his behaviour becomes progressively more social and 'better adjusted'. In this view, the fundamentals of social interaction are held to be cognitive. Social behaviour depends upon an underlying capacity to think, and its development can be understood in terms of the development of relevant forms of thought, amongst which role-taking inferences hold pride of place.

This approach is not without its critics, however. The individualism embodied in the approach has been attacked (Youniss, 1983), and the danger of over-intellectualization pointed out (Bearison, 1982; Glick, 1978). The main problem of social life, after all, is not to establish a theory of persons, but rather to *act* effectively.

The inherently individualistic conception of egocentrism as fixation in one's own point of view was criticized earlier in relation to visual perspective-taking. Piaget himself disavowed it in his comments on Vygotsky's *Thought and Language*: 'Egocentrism stems from a lack of differentiation between one's own point of view and other possible ones, and not at all from an individualism that precedes relations with others' (Piaget, 1962, p. 4). Youniss in fact takes us back to early Piaget to find the basis for a 'relational' approach. The idea that social development is mainly a matter of coming to know persons is mistaken, he argues. Persons are known, not as objects *per se*, but in terms of relations. Social knowledge is achieved through participation in orderly interactive relations with others. But how does the child enter into such relationships if not by dint of social knowledge? Youniss' answer seems to be that, from the outset, when the child acts the other *re*acts and the child thus cannot help but relate to the world via interpersonal relationships in which he is, willy nilly, engaged. 'Continued operation on their relation allows each subject to develop conceptions of one another as persons' (Youniss, 1978, p. 217).

This focus on relationships as prior to, and constitutive of, knowledge of persons provides the motif for a number of contemporary writers concerned with the 'construction' of the subject through discourse (e.g. Henriques *et al.*, 1984). Arguably there are many situations in which neither the relationship itself nor the participants themselves are explicitly represented as objects of reflection. Ongoing relationships provide a constant source of implicit definition of self and other.

Objective awareness of other, and of self, may be conceived as secondary to, and derivative from, a primary engagement in social relationships.

Recently students of social development have begun to show clear signs of rejecting the 'cognitive imperialism' inherent in the prevailing cognitive-developmental approach. For example Higgins, Ruble and Hartup (1983) present a number of papers which share a common concern to reassert the importance of experienced social interactions. One of the key concepts they offer towards an alternative approach is that of *scripts*. Scripts are 'general event representations' derived from, and applied to, social contexts. Adults are envisaged as providing the structure supporting their acquisition; children 'learn their parts' through participating in interaction. The emphasis is on the occurrence of fairly regular, generalizable patterns of interaction, into which the child is progressively drawn from a very early age. The child is thus enculturated into forms of relationship on the basis of more or less predictable and generalizable sequences of interaction.

Proponents of the script concept have tended to emphasize the efficiency inherent in 'scripted knowledge' – the use of scripts for oft-repeated encounters frees the individual's attention from other things. This of course applies as much to adults as to children. But developmentally, scripts may also provide an avenue into social behaviour which is relatively independent of sophisticated role-taking. Much social knowledge may be implicit in the scripted interaction without the child yet having appropriated that knowledge of himself. The development of explicit role-taking inferences may thus be envisaged as a gradual process of abstracting from patterns of interaction in which the child is already actively engaged.

Thus the prevailing hypothesis about the developmental relationship between role-taking and social interaction can be turned on its head. And this indeed is essentially what Mead originally envisaged. While role-taking has come to be seen as an ability which *underlies* social behaviour, Mead saw it as an activity which is implicit in it. Through social experience, he argued, role-taking is rendered increasingly explicit as a medium of reflective thought.

Mead's position on this finds clear echoes in much contemporary work on the development of thinking which emphasizes the developmental shift from implicit to explicit knowledge, from 'knowing how' to 'knowing that' (e.g. Lefebvre-Pinard, 1983; Robinson, 1983). The child's increasing awareness of others' perspectives implies increasing self-awareness and the achievement of some degree of objective detachment. The observer can be separated from the observed. In one form or another, whether couched in terms of 'disembedding' (Donaldson, 1978) or 'decontextualization' (Bruner, 1976) this has come to be seen as a central requirement for the emergence of logical thought.

So while it was the later Piagetian structuralist account of cognitive development which stimulated the explosion of role-taking research in the 1970s, recent developments are leading us back to the Piaget of the 1930s, and more especially to G.H. Mead. The rather one-sided pursuit of the cognitive underpinnings of social behaviour looks like being increasingly balanced by a growing interest in the social interactional antecedents of cognitive development. Although the concept of role-taking has strong associations with the former enterprise, it may soon find an equally important place within the latter.

References

Bearison, D., 'New directions in studies of social interaction and cognitive growth', in F. Serafica (ed.), *Social–Cognitive Development in Context*. London: Methuen, 1982.

Borke, H., 'The development of empathy in Chinese and American children between 3 and 6 years of age', *Developmental Psychology*, 1973, 9, 102–8.

Borke, H., 'Piaget's mountain's revisited: changes in the egocentric landscape', *Development Psychology*, 1975, 11, 240–3.

Bruner, J., 'Nature and uses of immaturity', in J.S. Bruner, A. Jolly and K. Sylva (eds), *Play: Its Role in Development and Evolution*. Harmondsworth: Penguin, 1976.

Buckley, N., Siegal, L., and Ness, S., 'Egocentrism, empathy and altruistic behaviour in young children', *Developmental Psychology*, 1979, 15, 329–30.

Chandler, M., 'Egocentrism and antisocial behaviour: the assessment and training of social perspective–talking skills', *Development Psychology*, 1973, 9, 326–32.

Chandler, M., 'Social cognition: a selective review of current research', in W. Overton and J. McCarthy Gallagher (eds), *Knowledge and Development*, Volume I: *Advances in Research and Theory*. New York: Plenum Press, 1977.

Chandler, M., Greenspan, S., and Barenboim, C., 'Assessment and training of role-taking and referential communication skills in institutionalized emotionally disturbed children', *Developmental Psychology*, 1974, 10, 546–53.

De Vries, R., 'The development of role-taking as reflected by the behaviour of bright, average and retarded children in a social guessing game', *Child Development*, 1970, 41, 759–70.

Donaldson, M., *Children's Minds*. London: Collins, 1978.

Eisenberg-Berg, N., and Lennon, R., 'Altruism and the assessment of empathy in the preschool years', *Child Development*, 1980, 51, 552–7.

Fishbein, H., Lewis, S., and Keiffer, K., 'Children's understanding of spatial relations: coordination of perspectives', *Developmental Psychology*, 1972, 7, 21–33.

Flavell, J., *The Development of Role-taking and Communication*. New York: Wiley, 1968.

Flavell, J., 'The development of inferences about others', in T. Mischel (ed.), *Understanding Other Persons*. Oxford: Blackwell, 1974.

Flavell, J., Abrahams Everett, B., Croft, K., and Flavell, J., 'Young children's knowledge about visual perception: further evidence for the Level 1 – Level 2 distinction', *Developmental Psychology*, 1981, 17, 99–103.

Ford, M., 'The construct validity of egocentrism', *Psychological Bulletin*, 1979, 86, 1169–88.

Freeman, N.H., and Cox, M.V. (eds), *Visual Order: the nature and development of pictorial representation*. Cambridge: Cambridge University Press, 1985.

Glick, J., 'Cognition and social cognition: an introduction', in J. Glick and A. Clarke-Stewart (eds), *The Development of Social Understanding*. New York: Gardner Press, 1978.

Henriques, J., Holloway, W., Urwin, C., Venn, C., Walkerdine, V., *Changing the Subject*. London: Methuen, 1984.

Higgins, E., 'Role-taking and social judgement: alternative developmental perspectives and process', in J. Flavell and J. Ross (eds), *Social Cognitive Development*. Cambridge: Cambridge University Press, 1981.

Higgins, E.T., Ruble, D., and Hartup, W. (eds), *Social Cognition and Social Development*. Cambridge: Cambridge University Press, 1983.

Hollos, M., 'Logical operations and role-taking abilities in two cultures: Norway and Hungary', *Child Development*, 1975, 46, 638–49.

Hudson, L., 'On the coherence of role-taking abilities: an alternative to correlational analysis', *Child Development*, 1978, 49, 223–7.

Hughes, M., 'Egocentrism in preschool children'. Unpublished PhD thesis, University of Edinburgh, 1975.

Hughes, M., and Donaldson, M., 'The use of hiding games for studying the coordination of viewpoints', *Educational Review*, 1979, 31, 133–40.

Hughes, M., and Donaldson, M., 'The use of hiding games for studying coordination of viewpoints', in M. Donaldson, R. Grieve, and C. Pratt (eds), *Early Child Development and Education*. Oxford: Blackwell, 1983.

Jennings, K., 'People vs. object orientation, social behaviour and intellectual abilities in preschool children', *Developmental Psychology*, 1975, 11, 511.

Johnson, D., 'Affective perspective-taking and cooperative disposition', *Developmental Psychology*, 1975, 11, 869–70.

Kohlberg, L., 'Moral stages and moralisation: the cognitive development approach', in T. Likona (ed.), *Moral Development and Behaviour*. New York: Holt, Rinehart & Winston, 1976.

Krauss, R., and Glucksberg, S., 'The development of communication competence as a function of age', *Child Development*, 1969, 40, 255–66.

Krebs, D., and Russell, C., 'Role-taking and altruism: when you put yourself in the shoes of another, will they take you to their owner's aid?', in J. Rushton and R. Sorrentino (eds), *Altruism and Helping Behaviour*, Volume II. Hillsdale, NJ: Erlbaum, 1980.

Kurdeck, L., 'Convergent validation of perspective-taking: a one-year follow up', *Developmental Psychology*, 1977, 13, 172–3.

Lefebvre-Pinard, M., 'Understanding and auto-control of cognitive functions: implications for the relationship between cognition and behaviour', *International Journal of Behaviour Development*, 1983, 6, 15–35.

Lempers, J., Flavell, E., and Flavell, J., 'The development in very young children of tacit knowledge concerning visual perception', *Genetic Psychology Monographs*, 1977, 95, 3–53.

Liben, L., and Belknap, B., 'Intellectual realism: implications for investigations of perceptual perspective taking in young children', *Child Development*, 1981, 52, 921–4.

Light, P.H., *The Development of Social Sensitivity*. Cambridge: Cambridge University Press, 1979.

Light, P.H., and Nix, C., '"Own view" versus "good view" in a perspective taking task', *Child Development*, 1983, 54, 480–3.

Light, P.H., and Simmons, B., 'The effect of a communication task upon the representation of depth relationships in young children's drawings', *Journal of Experimental Child Psychology*, 1983, 35, 81–92.

Maratsos, M., 'Nonegocentric communication abilities in preschool children', *Child Development*, 1973, 44, 697–700.

Marsh, D., Serafica, F., and Barenboim, C., 'Effect of perspective-taking training on interpersonal problem solving', *Child Development*, 1980, 51, 140–5.

Mead, G.H., *Mind, Self and Society*. Chicago: University of Chicago Press, 1934.

Miller, P., Kessel, F., and Flavell, J., 'Thinking about people thinking about . . .: a study of social cognitive development', *Child Development*, 1970, 41, 613–23.

Morss, J.R., 'Spatial egocentrism: the history of a Piagetian error'. Paper presented to the Annual Conference of the British Psychological Society, York, April 1983.

Mossler, D., Marvin, R., and Greenberg, M., 'Conceptual perspective taking in two to six year old children', *Developmental Psychology*, 1976, 12, 85–6.

Mussen, P., and Eisenberg-Berg, N., *Roots of Caring, Sharing and Helping: The Development of Prosocial Behaviour in Children*. San Francisco: Freeman, 1977.

O'Connor, M., 'The effect of role-taking training on role-taking and social behaviours in young children', *Social Behaviour and Personality*, 1977, 5, 1–11.

O'Reilly Landry, M., and Lyons Ruth, K., 'Recursive structure in cognitive perspective-taking', *Child Development*, 1980, 51, 386–94.

Payne, F., 'Children's prosocial conduct in structured situations and as viewed by others: consistency, convergence, and relationships with person variables', *Child Development*, 1980, 51, 1252–9.

Perner, J., Gruber, S., and Wimmer, H., 'Young children's conception of lying', *Cahiers de Psychologie Cognitive*, 1985, 5, 359–60.

Piaget, J., *The Language and Thought of the Child*. London: Routledge & Kegan Paul, 1926.

Piaget, J., *The Moral Judgement of the Child*. London: Routledge & Kegan Paul, 1932.

Piaget, J., *The Psychology of Intelligence*. London: Routledge & Kegan Paul, 1950.

Piaget, J., *Comments on Vygotsky's Critical Remarks*. Cambridge, Mass.: MIT Press, 1962.

Piaget, J., and Inhelder, B., *The Child's Conception of Space*. London: Routledge & Kegan Paul, 1956.

Piaget, J., and Inhelder, B., *The Psychology of the Child*. London: Routledge & Kegan Paul, 1969.

Robinson, E., 'Metacognitive development', in S. Meadows (ed.), *Developing Thinking*. London: Methuen, 1983.

Robinson, E., and Robinson, W., 'Egocentrism in verbal referential communication', in M. Cox (ed.), *Are Young Children Egocentric?* London: Batsford, 1980.

Rothenberg, B., 'Children's social sensitivity and the relationship to interpersonal competence, intrapersonal comfort and intellectual level', *Development Pschology*, 1970, 2, 335–50.

Rubin, K., 'Egocentrism in childhood: a unitary construct?', *Child Development*, 1973, 44, 102–10.

Rubin, K., 'Role-taking in childhood: some methodological considerations', *Child Development*, 1978, 49, 428–33.

Selman, R. (ed.), *The Growth of Interpersonal Understanding: Developmental and Clinical Analyses*. New York: Adademic Press, 1980.

Selman, R., Lavin, D., and Brion-Meisels, S., 'Troubled children's use of self–reflection', in F. Serafica (ed.), *Social-Cognitive Development in Context*. London: Methuen, 1982.

Shure, M., 'Interpersonal problem solving: a cog in the wheel of social cognition', in F. Serafica (ed.), *Social-Cognitive Development in Context*. London: Methuen, 1982.

Urberg, K., and Docherty, E., 'Development of role-taking skills in young children', *Developmental Psychology*, 1976, 12, 198–203.

Van Lieshout, C., Leckie, G., and Smits-Van Sonsbeek, B., 'Social perspective-taking, training and role-taking ability of preschool children', in K. Riegel and J. Meacham (eds) *The Developing Individual in a Changing World, Volume II: Social and Environmental Issues*. The Hague, Mouton, 1976.

Youniss, J., 'The nature of social development: a conceptual discussion of cognition', in H. McGurk (ed.), *Issues in Childhood Social Development*. London: Methuen, 1978.

Youniss, J., 'Piaget and the self-constituted through relations', in W. Overton (ed.), *The Relationship Between Social and Cognitive Development*. Hillsdale, NJ: Erlbaum, 1983.

Zahn-Waxler, C., Radke-Yarrow, M., and Brady-Smith, J., 'Perspective-taking and prosocial behaviour', *Developmental Psychology*, 1977, 13, 87–8.

3
Some benefits of egocentrism
GEORGE BUTTERWORTH

We are in danger of misjudging young children if we compare their faculties with the final goal to which their development is directed. A child is considered more nearly perfect, the nearer he approaches this goal. The earlier stages appear to be imperfect, even inferior, because they are compared with functional ability accomplished later instead of with the demands appropriate for the age. Actually however, every child born maturely is a perfect being in himself at every stage of his development and is always adjusted admirably to his natural surroundings. Otherwise, mankind would have become extinct long ago. (A. Peiper, 1963, p. 597)

Introduction

The remarkable growth in our appreciation of the cognitive competence of infants and young children that has been the result of the intensive research efforts of recent years surely requires a reappraisal of some basic concepts in developmental psychology. The most immediate effect of this progress within the discipline may be to lead us to abandon concepts because our new knowledge makes more 'primitive' psychologies outdated. On such grounds it might be argued that the contemporary status of egocentrism in developmental psychology is similar to that of phlogiston in the history of chemistry. It is a concept that has had its day, one that our new, scientific developmental psychology can do without.

Another approach however may be to revise fundamental theoretical concepts in the light of the new evidence, so that what is valuable may be retained while misconceptions are corrected. The latter approach is beginning to find expression in recent literature (e.g. Morss, 1983; Cox, 1985) and a plea for the general utility of the concept of egocentrism has already been made elsewhere (Butterworth, 1980, 1983). The aim here will be to extend our understanding of this basic concept by examining evidence on perception and cognition in very young infants that may throw light on the adaptive function of egocentrism, both for the development of self-awareness and in social cognition.

Piaget (1926) first proposed egocentrism to be the defining characteristic of the language and thought of the child. He presented it as a negative aspect of childhood, a state of mind that we must grow out of in order that we may perceive ourselves and others in the world as we 'really are'. Perhaps because Piaget was so concerned to explain how the child's knowledge is slowly perfected in development the emphasis has inevitably been on the child's need to 'escape' from egocentrism. With the exception of Vygotsky (1962), who seriously disagreed with Piaget on the role of egocentric speech in the development of thought, theorists have usually cast egocentrism in a negative light so that what it may actually enable in the cognitive development of the child has been overlooked.

The aim of this chapter is to reconsider the origins of egocentrism in relation to contemporary evidence on perception in human infants. The account will be restricted to two lines of research that illuminate basic errors in the traditional definition. The first set of studies will show that even very young babies have access to and can make use of information that specifies a distinction between 'self' and 'environment'; a second set of studies will be considered that show infants to perceive differences between their own and another's point of view. The implications for the standard concept of egocentrism, defined as an inability to differentiate subject and object, or to be aware of the experiences of another, will be considered. It will be argued that 'egocentrism' may reflect the psychological point of origin of unreflective, everyday experience. This need not mean that the experience itself is unreliable, or cannot be communicated. On the contrary, the important implication of a reappraisal of perception as the most basic 'egocentric' cognitive process is that it may reveal a pre-reflective level of direct awareness of the environment which we do not grow out of but to which we may refer our elaborated hypotheses as they develop.

Defining egocentrism

The concept of egocentrism is not at all an easy one to define exhaustively but there are two esential aspects. These are (i) a spatial component concerning the point of origin of experience, and (ii) non-differentiation of the subject and object of experience. In an attempt to capture Piaget's use of the term, Flavell (1963) defined the concept as follows:

> Egocentrism denotes a cognitive state in which the cognizer sees the world from a single point of view only, his own but without knowledge of the existence of viewpoints or perspectives and without awareness that he is a prisoner of his own [viewpoint]. (p. 60)

Further definitions offered by Piaget include the following:

> It is somehow the totality of pre-critical and pre-objective attitudes of knowledge.

> Undifferentiation between the other and the self.

> It consists only in taking as sole reality the one which appears to perception.
>   (quotations from Piaget published in Battro, 1973)

These further definitions make it clear that lack of differentiation from the physical and social environment is fundamental to the Piagetian interpretation of egocentrism; egocentrism leads the child to rely on the fallible and self-centred impressions of immediate experience. Egocentrism stands mid-way between individualized and socialized thought. It stems from a lack of differentiation between one's own point of view and other possible points of view, and from dependence upon immediate sensory impressions considered by Piaget to be unreliable indices of the true nature of reality.

Some problems with Piaget's assumptions on the origins of egocentrism

The fundamental problem with Piaget's definition of egocentrism concerns his assumptions about the initial adaptation of the infant to the environment. Piaget's account of the developmental relationship between perceiving, acting and knowing is based on the premise that there is no information in the structure of stimulus information itself that would enable response-contingent feedback to be distinguished from sensory data that is independent of the infant's own behaviour. Here we may go straight to the heart of the matter because Piaget puts at the roots of childhood egocentrism a profound and complete 'adualism' between infant and world. There is nothing in Piaget's theory of sensory perception to inform the infant of an objective independent reality nor is there anything to render the mind of another transparent to the child. The fundamental problem is that Piaget offers a totally constructionist account of cognitive development such that even the most elementary levels of experience require construction through action (during infancy) or through the operations of the intellect (in later childhood). Piaget's is a 'representationalist' theory of perception, as opposed to the 'presentationalist' theories of direct perception such as that propounded by Gibson (1966). Since perception on Piaget's view is always mediated, this precludes perception of either physical or social objects before the appropriate mental structures have been constructed in the course of repeated motor activities (the object concept, concepts of space, time and causality). On this theory the infant is locked into a private world. The notion that egocentrism consists in 'taking as the sole reality the one that appears to perception' in Piaget's usage emphasizes the private, incoherent, unreliable and subjective nature of experience before knowledge has been acquired.

Recent studies however have amassed a great deal of

evidence that Piaget's assumptions about the nature of early sensory perception may have been wrong (for reviews see Bower, 1982; Butterworth, 1981; Harris, 1983). In general the evidence on early infant perception is more consistent with a 'presentationalist' than a 'representationalist' realist position; that is, infants behave as if they have direct access to the real world in a variety of contexts when tested for their responses to sensory information. Just to list a few examples: newborn infants are sensitive to the patterning of auditory stimulation and will co-locate auditory and visual stimuli which share common rhythmic properties (Spelke, 1983; Butterworth and Castillo, 1976); 3-month-old infants are sensitive to the invariant relation between aspects of phonetic structure and the visual information conveyed by the mouth positions involved in the articulation of sounds (Kuhl and Meltzoff, 1982); neonates imitate mouth opening and tongue protrusion, an ability that requires perception of abstract invariants relating visual information to motor output (Meltzoff 1981; Vynter, 1983); 5-month-old infants use information obtained from dynamic transitions in optical texture that occur during the relative motions of objects to make spatial discriminations that enable them to perceive occlusion of one object by another (Granrud *et al.*, 1984, Kellman and Spelke, 1983). All of these discriminations are available to perception long before the child could have constructed the motor schemes Piaget considered necessary, and they may be taken as evidence against his constructivist theory.

We may now elaborate the argument for redefining egocentrism in the context of two lines of research which illustrate its basic aspects. The first set of studies will show that even very young infants have access to, and can make use of, information that specifies a distinction between 'self' and 'environment'. The implications for the standard definition of egocentrism as an inability to differentiate subject and object will be reviewed. A second set of studies will be considered which shows that infants perceive that others share points of view on the world. The implications for the definition of egocentrism as an inability to be aware of the experience of another will be outlined.

The problem of adualism

According to Piaget, the initial relationship between the infant and the environment is one of profound adualism. In his theory there is no information inherent in the structure of sensory stimulation itself to allow the infant to distinguish between action-contingent sensory changes and events that occur independently of the actions of the perceiver. This assumption forms the most basic aspect of Piaget's concept of egocentrism, since it presupposes a complete lack of differentiation between infant and the environment as the starting point for development. On Piaget's theory of perception a distinction between self as an object of experience and independent objects in the world is only slowly established through laborious construction of sensori-motor coordinations and the development of representation during the first 18 months of life. By contrast, Michotte (1950) and more recently Gibson (1966, 1979) have presented alternative accounts of perception which stress that there is information within the sensory array sufficient to specify a distinction between observer and observed. If such information exists, and if very young infants can be shown to make use of it, then the assumption that development begins from a state of complete adualism may need to be revised.

Recent research on the infant's perception of object occlusion has already been mentioned briefly. The importance of such work is that it illustrates how very much infant perception depends upon dynamic transitions in continuous sensory stimulation. From complex properties of incoming sensory stimulation the infant can pick up objective information concerning the relationship between self and environment. Much of the research on object permanence demonstrates that whether an object is perceived as 'temporarily occluded' or as 'annihilated' after it passes out of sight depends on dynamic transitions that occur in visual information at the moment when an object disappears. Babies may not be subject to the 'egocentric' fallacy that an object exists solely as an extension of their own actions.

Bower (1967) and more recently Kellman and Spelke (1983) showed that an object which is temporarily occluded is correctly perceived as 'invisible but present' by infants between

2 and 4 months of age. The latter study strongly implicated texture deletion, dynamic information arising from the movement of the occluded object as it passes behind the occluding screen, in the perception of permanence. A recent study by Granrud *et al.* (1984) also strongly implicated dynamic information obtained by progressive deletion of texture in perception on depth among 5-month-old infants. A random-dot display generated by computer used texture deletion to create the appearance of depth at an edge on the surface of a video monitor. The effect is to make one part of the picture seem to lie 'in front of' the remainder. Infants would reach preferentially towards that part of the computer display that appeared to be nearer to them, as specified by the relations of occlusion in the textured display. Spelke (1983) showed that real objects separated in depth and undergoing relative motion to each other also elicit preferential reaching in babies at about 5 months. Babies therefore appear to be using texture deletion information from movement, obtained by direct perception, to inform them of a world of spatially connected, separately moveable, whole, permanent objects in the first 5 months of life. Objects are perceived as independent of self and as possessing properties of permanence and substantiality long before these could have been constructed through the circular reactions.

Not only do babies appear to perceive object permanence through dynamic transitions in the optic array, but such transitions may also serve to inform the baby about its own body as an object of experience. Newborn babies make defensive responses to a looming stimulus that has been produced by accelerated expansion of a delimited portion of the visual field, as if on a collision course with the baby (Bower, Broughton and Moore, 1970; Ball and Tronick, 1971). That is, the baby seems to defend its own body against the approaching object, a phenomenon that seems to indicate that the infant innately differentiates between self and object.

The most revealing evidence against the hypothesis that development begins in a state of profound adualism, however, comes from studies in which the infant's postural stability is studied under conditions where there is total movement of the optic array. Gibson (1966) coined the term 'visual proprioception' to draw attention to the role of vision in providing information for self-movement through perspective transformations of the retinal image that arise when an observer moves through a stable visual space. The direction of movement of the observer is specified by total motion of a structured visual array, outward from a stationary central point. Under conditions of the natural ecology (where the surroundings may be considered stable) such a flow pattern can only arise when the observer is moving; hence it is sufficient to specify the distinction between 'self' and 'the world'. Gibson argued that such flow patterns are given in the structure of sensory information itself. The developing child need only attend to the available information; there is no necessity to construct the invariants. However, until the early 1970s there was little empirical information that would enable the Gibsonian and Piagetian accounts to be separated. It seemed possible that optic flow patterns might equally gain their significance through the infant's developing mobility (and hence be constructed through action) as to be inherently informative, as Gibson maintained.

Lee and Aronson (1974) were the first to show that infants use visual information to monitor their posture. Babies who had recently learned to stand were tested standing on a rigid floor, within a moveable room comprising three walls and a ceiling. The infants faced the interior end wall and the whole structure, except the floor, was moved so that the end wall slowly approached or receded. Babies compensated for a non-existent loss of balance signalled by the optic flow pattern (generated by the movement of the surroundings) and consequently fell in the direction appropriate to the plane of instability specified by the misleading visual flow pattern. If the end wall moved away from the baby, the infant fell forward and if the wall moved towards the baby, the infant fell over backwards.

Subsequent studies demonstrated that vision does not acquire its proprioceptive function as a result of motor development. Butterworth and Hicks (1977) found that infants too young to walk would nevertheless compensate for visually specified instability when seated in the moving room. Butterworth and Cicchetti (1978) showed that length of experience of the sitting or standing posture in babies was negatively correlated with susceptibility to misleading visual feedback.

The maximum disruption by discrepant visual feedback occurred during the period of three months after each posture was acquired and declined thereafter. The research has been extended to pre-locomotor infants by Pope (1984) who showed that even before babies can crawl they are responsive to discrepant visual feedback. Infants as young as 2 months, when supported in an infant chair, will make directionally appropriate compensatory movements of the head under conditions of discrepant visual feedback. Pope (1984) showed that the onset of independent locomotion by crawling, at about 6 months, actually coincides with a relative decline in susceptibility to the effects of misleading visual feedback in the moving room.

The pattern of high susceptibility to the optic flow pattern is repeated when the child starts to walk. With the onset of bipedal locomotion, the infant once again becomes very unstable in the face of misleading visual feedback as control over the unfamiliar standing posture is acquired. After about three months of extreme instability, there is a decline in the effects of moving the room as autonomous control is gained (Butterworth and Cicchetti, 1978). Information arriving in the periphery of vision is particularly implicated in postural control since movement of just the central portion of the visual field does not generate instability in babies who have recently learned to stand (Pope, 1984). Far from independent locomotion giving rise to meaningful optic flow patterns, the infant appears to make use of the optic flow pattern as a means of gaining control over the body in its succession of postures so that when locomotion does ensue, the infant will be assured of a degree of autonomous control. The implication is that the optic flow pattern is inherently informative about the relation between the infant and the environment. A boundary exists in infant perception between infant and the world such that the absolute 'adualism' assumed by Piaget is not supported.

What are the implications for egocentrism? Studies of the kind discussed above go to the heart of the matter, since it is clear that Piaget's theory of development beginning from a state of 'absolute' egocentrism, of complete 'adualistic confusion', cannot explain such observations. It becomes necessary to reconsider the role of sensory perception in cognitive growth, since from the earliest age the infant seems to make distinctions at the level of perception that Piaget had considered a function of cognitive development during the first year of life. On the other hand, it is clear that the very young infant has no objective, reflective self-knowledge. In the 'moving room' studies, even though the infant is objectively stable, postural compensations are made to the misleading visual feedback. It is not until infants are about 15 months of age that they have developed sufficient reflective self-awareness to turn to see 'who has made the room move' (Butterworth and Cicchetti, 1978). For many months in the first year, the infant behaves as if completely dependent on the information available to perception. But this makes sense, and is perfectly adaptive since under normal conditions, where the ground can be considered stable, self-motion is specified in movement-contingent optic flow patterns which incorporate an implicit distinction between self and surround. Even under conditions of passive movement the distinction between observer and observed is imposed by the normal ecology and does not need to be constructed *de novo* in development as Piaget had assumed (for a fuller discussion see Butterworth, 1981, pp. 144–50).

If these arguments are accepted, then it is clear that development does not begin from an absolute adualism. Even at the most basic levels of cognitive functioning there is an implicit distinction between observer and observed, between self and environment. Although the infant must rely on the data of sensory experience for cognitive development, this does not mean that the baby is at the mercy of entirely subjective impressions, as Piaget had supposed.

Taking the point of view of another person

We may take this argument further by considering the implications of recent research for Piaget's definition of egocentrism as an inability to appreciate another's point of view. Morss (1983) points out that historically Piaget's concept of childhood egocentrism is closely linked with the psychoanalytic concept of autism, introduced by Bleuler and Jung, to characterize unconscious thought processes of a strictly personal and incommunicable kind. By extrapolation backwards into infancy, Piaget developed a 'strong' form of egocentrism that brings together narcissim, autism and solipsism in the 'ontolo-gical egocentrism' of the sensori-motor period. He presents a picture of the very young infant as totally locked into a private and incommunicable world unaware of the viewpoints of others.

It was therefore something of a milestone in the developmen-tal psychology of infancy when Scaife and Bruner (1975) noted that infants from 2 months of age adjust their line of gaze in response to a change in the focus of attention of an adult. Since the baby reorients its own visual attention on the basis of a change in the point of view of another person, Scaife and Bruner argued that infants must be less than totally egocentric. Subsequent studies have confirmed this result and extended our knowledge of how 'joint attention' is possible between adult and baby. Schaffer (1984) reviews a number of experi-ments carried out in his laboratory; he points out that gaze exerts a powerful signalling effect and mothers very readily follow their infants' gaze to maintain mutual attention to shared topics. Joint attention serves an important purpose in early communication and in the mother's attempts at tutoring the infant.

The theoretical importance of visual coorientation for our understanding of egocentrism, however, lies in the reciprocal nature of the phenomenon. Not only does the mother make use of the infant's line of gaze to establish joint visual attention but also the infant is well able to redirect his or her own gaze to share in the focus of the mother's attention.

Butterworth and Cochran (1980) and Butterworth and Jarrett (1980) carried out an extensive series of studies in an attempt to establish how a baby can know where someone else is looking. The studies were carried out under strictly controlled condi-tions in an undistracting environment, with identical targets placed at various positions relative to the mother and infant. These conditions allow unambiguous conclusions to be drawn about the infant's ability to single out the referent of the adult's gaze.

Evidence was obtained for three successive 'stages', between the ages of 6 and 18 months, in the development of mechanisms of joint visual attention. At 6 months of age, infants will look to the correct side of the room, as if to see what the mother is looking at, but they cannot tell *on the basis of the mother's action alone* which of two identical targets the mother is attending to. Even with large angular separations of 60 degrees between the targets, although they are accurate for targets first along their scan path they are at chance level when the correct target is second along the scan path. Furthermore, infants will only localize targets within their own visual field. If the mother looks at a target located behind the baby, the infant either fixates a target in front and within the visual field or will not respond. At 6 months joint visual attention certainly is restricted to locations within the baby's range of immediate visual perception. The mechanism involved at 6 months we have called 'ecological', since we believe that accurate joint visual attention at this age depends not only on the mother's signal but also on the intrinsic differentiating properties of the object being attended by the mother. Where the targets are identical, as in Figure 3.1, the infant cannot tell which is the referent. However, where the correct target singles itself out in some way, perhaps through movement or some other attention-worthy characteristic, then the 'reference triangle' (Ogden and Richards, 1938) between adult, infant and the object will be satisfactorily completed. Figure 3.1 illustrates the pattern of performance of 6-month infants in one of our studies in which four identical targets were presented at various locations in the room, relative to the mother and baby.

By 12 months however, the infant is beginning to localize the targets correctly whether first or second along the scan path, even though the targets are identical. The only information allowing this is the angular displacement of the mother's head and eye movement. This mechanism we have called 'geometric' since it seems to involve extrapolation of an invisible line along the mother's line of gaze to the target, as in the geometric process of triangulation. However, the child is still limited to targets within the field of vision and will not accurately locate targets behind, even if the room in front of the baby is completely devoid of alternative targets. Figure 3.2 illustrates the data for 12-month babies in the same experimental situation as previously discussed (four identical targets at various locations in the room).

The geometric mechanism is definitely available at 18

74   *Making Sense*

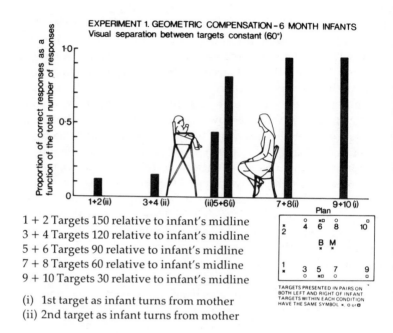

EXPERIMENT 1. GEOMETRIC COMPENSATION – 6 MONTH INFANTS
Visual separation between targets constant (60°)

1 + 2 Targets 150 relative to infant's midline
3 + 4 Targets 120 relative to infant's midline
5 + 6 Targets 90 relative to infant's midline
7 + 8 Targets 60 relative to infant's midline
9 + 10 Targets 30 relative to infant's midline

(i) 1st target as infant turns from mother
(ii) 2nd target as infant turns from mother

TARGETS PRESENTED IN PAIRS ON
BOTH LEFT AND RIGHT OF INFANT
TARGETS WITHIN EACH CONDITION
HAVE THE SAME SYMBOL ×, o or □

Figure 3.1 Geometric compensation – 6-month infants
Visual separation between targets constant (60°)
Source: Butterworth, 1982

months, as Figure 3.3 illustrates. Babies are equally accurate whether the target is first or second along the scan path, yet they still remain virtually restricted to the targets within their own visual field when targets remain in view. However, if all targets are removed from the field of view, then 18-month infants will turn and locate targets behind them when the mother looks in that direction. This suggests that by 18 months the spatial boundaries for joint visual reference have been extended beyond the field of immediate vision to a represented space, within with the infant conceives self and objects to be co-located.

These experiments have provided a framework for an extensive appraisal of the nature of egocentrism in babies and the mechanisms of infant-adult communication. One effect of the research has been to lead to an understanding of the importance of 'distractibility' for the processes of communica-

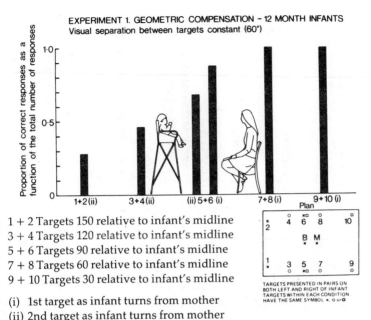

EXPERIMENT 1. GEOMETRIC COMPENSATION – 12 MONTH INFANTS
Visual separation between targets constant (60°)

1 + 2 Targets 150 relative to infant's midline
3 + 4 Targets 120 relative to infant's midline
5 + 6 Targets 90 relative to infant's midline
7 + 8 Targets 60 relative to infant's midline
9 + 10 Targets 30 relative to infant's midline

(i) 1st target as infant turns from mother
(ii) 2nd target as infant turns from mother

TARGETS PRESENTED IN PAIRS ON
BOTH LEFT AND RIGHT OF INFANT
TARGETS WITHIN EACH CONDITION
HAVE THE SAME SYMBOL ×, ○ or □

Figure 3.2 Geometric compensation – 12-month infants
Visual separation between targets constant (60°)
Source: Butterworth, 1982

tion with a very young baby. Although the infant below 9 or 10 months cannot isolate the referent of the mother's gaze *on the basis of the angular displacement of the mother's head alone*, this does not mean that true joint attention is impossible. Our hypothesis is that the earlier mechanism of joint attention, the 'ecological' mechanism as we have called it, depends on the distractibility of the infant. Communication occurs because the easily distractible young infant attends not only to the signal value of the mother's change of visual orientation, but thereafter to the attention compelling features of objects in the environment. The young infant's distractibility, when seen in social context, may be explained as a basic means of entering into a communication network through the *intrinsically* attention-compelling features of publicly shared objects. What from one point of view may be seen as a cognitive limitation turns out to be an asset when seen in ecological terms.

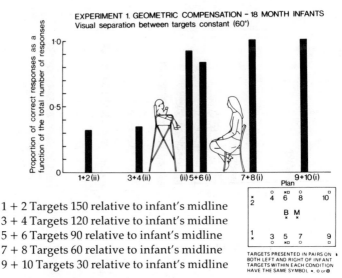

1 + 2 Targets 150 relative to infant's midline
3 + 4 Targets 120 relative to infant's midline
5 + 6 Targets 90 relative to infant's midline
7 + 8 Targets 60 relative to infant's midline
9 + 10 Targets 30 relative to infant's midline

(i)   1st target as infant turns from mother
(ii) 2nd target as infant turns from mother

Figure 3.3 Geometric compensation – 18-month infants
Visual separation between targets constant (60°)
Source: Butterworth, 1982

Communication, through intrinsic attention mechanisms, emerges as one rather unsuspected benefit of egocentrism.

Superimposed on this basic mechanism, with cognitive development, comes precise 'geometric' localization of the referent of the mother's gaze. Incidentally, this mechanism need not be considered to supplant the ecological one as a traditional stage theory might suppose. Rather, the availability of a 'geometric' means of locating the referent of the mother's gaze may be considered to lessen the ambiguity of reference (even though it can never totally remove it). Finally, by about 18 months the geometric mechanism applies not only to visual space but also to a represented space. The 18-month infant can conceive of a space within which he or she is contained together with other objects potentially available to joint attention with an adult.

What are the more general implications of this research for egocentrism? On the one hand, the fact that infants respond at all to a change in the mother's gaze might suggest non-egocentrism on the argument that it is a change *in another person's point of view* that has led the infant to respond. On the other hand, since under circumstances where the mother looks behind the baby the infant assimilates her line of regard to his or her own visual field, this might be taken as evidence for egocentrism. (As discussed above, when mother looks behind the baby the infant up to 12 months terminates visual search at about 40 degrees from the midline if the field of view is empty or picks out a target in the visual field). To resolve this paradox it is necessary to move away from a solipsistic account of visual perception towards a theory of direct realism in infant visual perception.

A theory of direct perception, such as that propounded by Gibson (1966) can resolve the paradox suggested by these results. Perception necessarily involves a point of view but this need not preclude an ability to perceive that others also have a perspective on a space that can be common to several points of view. Joint visual attention is ultimately possible because visual perception presupposes a world of objects that exist in a common, external space. The results suggest that the young infant's ability to share objects of attention with another is limited by the boundaries of her own visual field. To respond to signals directed at objects outside the boundaries of immediate perception may require the development of a represented space but this will only extend the boundaries of the space already available in immediate perception. Concepts of objects and of space may not be necessary for perceiving that others also have points of view. An elementary intersubjective process of this kind ultimately works because the perceptual systems of different individuals function in basically the same way, so that even if the cognitive development of the participants in the interaction is at very different levels, the processes of immediate perception provide a basis for intersubjective agreement on the objects of experience.

Conclusion

The implication of all the research that has been reviewed above is that if egocentrism consists in 'taking as the sole reality the one that appears to perception', when the child falls back on direct experience, or relies on context to disambiguate an event not fully understood, it falls back on a level of experience which provides the most intimate contact with reality. Egocentrism is not a retreat into privacy or solipsism but arises because the child falls back on the objectivity of experience, on the externality and shared data of sensory perception, where more abstract means of knowing have failed or are simply not yet available.

The implication of this analysis is that the phenomena commonly described as 'egocentric' in the literature on children's cognitive development may simply occur because the child relies on the data of unreflective perception where appropriate knowledge is lacking. Although attention may not be directed to the most appropriate aspect of the environment by the naive child, this need not mean that the information obtained through perception is unreliable or that it cannot be communicated. Perception may constitute the most basic of the cognitive processes that contribute to development but it is only egocentric in the limited sense of its point of origin. The information available to the child from a particular position need not be peculiar to that position but may also be available from a variety of other viewpoints. In social situations the child's difficulty may lie in isolating the specific referent of another's attention, among the variety of possible referents. rather than in Piaget's supposition that the child has difficulty in comprehending the possibility of other points of view.

Among other benefits a revaluation of the concept of egocentrism along these lines may lead us to think of innate sensibilities to the informative properties of sensory stimulation, such as optic flow patterns brought about by motion in relation to a textured ground as revealing a 'programming language' for the development of reflective self-awareness. Such a revaluation of the concept of egocentrism also makes *theoretically* possible intersubjectivity between the naive infant and the cognitively sophisticated adult. This pre-reflective level of awareness may correspond to a mode of psychological functioning that we do not grow out of but to which, even as adults, we may refer our abstract hypotheses when we seek verification or refutation.

References

Ball, W., and Tronick, E., 'Infant responses to impending collision, optical and real', *Science*, 1971, 171, 818–20.

Battro, A.M., *Piaget: Dictionary of Terms*. Oxford: Pergamon Press, 1973.

Bower, T.G.R., 'The development of object permanence: some studies of existence constancy', *Perception and Psychophysics*, 1967, 2, 411–18.

Bower, T.G.R., *Development in Infancy* (2nd edn). San Francisco: Freeman, 1982.

Bower, T.G.R., Broughton, J., and Moore, M.K., 'Infant responses to approaching objects: an indicator of response to distal variables', *Perception and Psychophysics*, 1970, 9, 193–6.

Butterworth, G.E., 'A discussion of some issues raised by Piaget's concept of childhood egocentrism', in M.V. Cox (ed.), *Are Young Children Egocentric?* London: Batsford, 1980.

Butterworth, G.E., 'Object permanence and identity in Piaget's theory of infant cognition', in G.E. Butterworth (ed.), *Infancy and Epistemology*. Brighton: Harvester, 1981.

Butterworth, G.E., 'Structure of the mind in human infancy', in Lipsitt, L. (ed.) *Advances in Infancy Research*, Volume 2, 1–29. Norwood, New Jersey: Ablex, 1982.

Butterworth, G.E., 'Social cognition: the case for Piaget', in S. Modgil, C. Modgil and G. Brown (eds), *Jean Piaget: An Interdisciplinary Critique*. London: Routledge & Kegan Paul, 1983.

Butterworth, G.E., and Castillo, M., 'Coordination of auditory and visual space in newborn human infants', *Perception*, 1976, 5, 155–60.

Butterworth, G.E., and Cicchetti, D., 'Visual calibration of posture in normal and motor retarded Down's syndrome infants,' *Perception*, 1978, 7, 513–25.

Butterworth, G.E., and Cochran, E.C., 'Towards a mechanism of joint visual attention in human infancy', *International Journal of Behavioural Development*, 1980, 3, 253–72.

Butterworth, G.E., and Hicks, L., 'Visual proprioception and postural stability in infancy: a developmental study', *Perception*, 1977, 6, 255–62.

Butterworth, G.E., and Jarrett, N., 'The geometry of pre-verbal communication'. Paper presented to the Developmental Psychology Section of the British Psychological Society, Edinburgh, 1980.

Cox, M., *The Child's Point of View*. Brighton: Harvester, 1985.

Flavell, J.H., *The Developmental Psychology of Jean Piaget*. London: Van Nostrand, 1963.

Gibson, J.J., *The Senses Considered as Perceptual Systems*. Boston: Houghton-Mifflin, 1966.

Gibson, J.J., *The Ecological Approach to Visual Perception*. Boston: Houghton-Mifflin, 1979.

Granrud, C.E., Yonas, A., Smith, I.M., Arterberry, M.E., Glicksman, M.L., and Sorkness, A.C., 'Infants' sensitivity to accretion and deletion of texture as information for depth at an edge', *Child Development*, 1984, 55, 1630–6.

Harris, P.L., 'Infant cognition', in M.M. Haith (ed.), *Handbook of Child Psychology*, Volume II: *Infancy and Biological Development*. New York: Wiley, 1983.

Kellman, P.J., and Spelke, E.S., 'Perception of partly occluded objects in infancy', *Cognitive Psychology*, 1983, 15, 483–524.

Kuhl, P., and Meltzoff, A.N., 'The bimodal perception of speech in infancy', *Science*, 1982, 218, 1138–41.

Lee, D., and Aronson, E., 'Visual proprioceptive control of standing in human infants', *Perception and Psychophysics*, 1974, 15, 529–32.

Meltzoff, A.N., 'Imitation, intermodal coordination and representation in early infancy', in G.E. Butterworth (ed.), *Infancy and Epistemology: An Evaluation of Piaget's Theory*. Brighton: Harvester, 1981.

Michotte, A., 'A propos de la permanence phenomenale, faits et theories', *Acta Psychologica*, 1950, 7, 298–322.

Morss, J.R., 'Spatial egocentrism, the history of a Piagetian error'. Paper presented to the Annual Conference of the British Psychological Society, York, April 1983.

Ogden, C.K., and Richards, I.A., *The Meaning of Meaning*. London: Kegan Paul, Trench, Trubner & Co., 1938.

Peiper, A., *Cerebral Function in Infancy and Childhood*. New York: Consultants Bureau, 1963.

Piaget, J., *The Language and Thought of the Child*. New York: Harcourt Brace, 1926.

Pope, M.J., 'Development of visual proprioception'. Unpublished PhD thesis, University of Southampton, 1984.

Scaife, M., and Bruner, J.S., 'The capacity for joint visual attention in the infant', *Nature*, 1975, 253, 265.

Schaffer, H.R., *The Child's Entry into a Social World*. London: Academic Press, 1984.

Spelke, E.S., *Cognition in Infancy*. Occasional Paper no. 23, Center for Cognitive Science, Massachusetts Institute of Technology, 1983.

Vygotsky, L.S., *Thought and Language*. Cambridge, Mass.: MIT Press, 1962.

Vynter, A., 'Imitation, prepresentation et mouvement dans les premieres mois de la vie'. Unpublished PhD thesis, University of Geneva, 1983.

4

The transactional self

JEROME BRUNER

If you engage for long in the study of how human beings relate
to one another, especially through the use of language, you are
bound to be struck by the importance of 'transactions'. This is
not an easy word to define. I want to signify those dealings
which are premised on a mutual sharing of assumptions and
beliefs about how the world is, how mind works, what we are
up to, and how communication should proceed. It is an idea
captured to some extent by Paul Grice's maxims about how to
proceed in conversation, by Deirdre Wilson and Dan Sperber's
notion that we always assume that what others have said must
make some sense, by Hilary Putnam's recognition that we
usually assign the right level of ignorance or cleverness to our
interlocutors. Beyond these specifics, there remains a shady but
important area of sharing – Colwyn Trevarthen calls it 'intersubjectivity' – that makes the philosopher's query about how
we know Other Minds seem more practical than the philosopher ever intended it to be.

One knows intuitively as a psychologist (or simply as a
human being) that the easy access we have into each other's
minds, not so much in the particulars of what we are thinking
but in general about what minds are like, cannot be explained
away by invoking singular concepts like 'empathy'. Nor does it
seem sufficient to perform a miracle of phenomenology, as did
the German philosopher Max Scheler, and subdivide *Einfuhlung*

into a half-dozen 'feelable' classes. Or to take the route of nineteeth-century psychologists and elevate 'sympathy' to the status of an instinct. More typically, the contemporary student of mind will try to unravel the mystery by exploring how we develop this sense of what other minds are about, or by examining its pathologies, as in autistic children and in young schizophrenics. Or he will try to unravel the details of interpersonal knowledge among adults by conducting experiments on facets of this knowledge, as have Fritz Heider and his students. Or, yet another alternative, he will dismiss the issue of intersubjective knowledge as 'nothing but' projection, for whatever smug satisfaction that may give him.

I first became caught up in this issue through work I did in collaboration with Renato Tagiuri, and we ended up writing a chapter on 'person perception' in one of the standard hand-books – treating it as a perceptual problem. Along the way to that chapter we did some of those little experiments which are the craft of psychology. We asked people who were parts of small groups or cliques and who knew each other well two very simple questions: who in the group would they (each individual) most like to spend more time with, and who in the group did they think would most like to spend more time with them. I should say at the outset that this is a procedure fraught with statistical problems, particularly if one wants to study the 'accuracy' of interpersonal perceptions or to determine whether people's choices are 'trans parent' to others. But the statistical hurdles can be jumped by using what are called 'Monte Carlo procedures', which consist of allocating each person's choices and guesses of others' choices with the aid of a roulette wheel. One can then compare the subjects' real performance with the wheel's allocation of choices and guesses by chance. Yes, on average people are more accurate and more transparent than would be expected by chance – a not very startling finding. They know better than chance who likes them, or to put it inversely, people's preferences are transparent.

But there is something very curious about how people operate in such situations that is not so obvious after all. For one thing, a person who chooses another will (in excess of chance) believe that the other person chooses him back. Or, since the direction of cause is never clear in human affairs, if we feel chosen by somebody, we will choose that person in return whether our feeling is correct or not. There is simply a human bias: feeling liked by somebody begets liking him back. To this add the fact that we know better than chance who likes us. Now, is this a matter of 'accuracy' or of 'vanity'? Are we 'victims' of vanity or beneficiaries of our sensitivity? If we bias our Monte Carlo wheels with these same 'human' tendencies, they will perform indistinguishably from humans. Does that mean that humans are simply biased robots? It that a meaningful question, really? It smacks altogether too much of those early Cartesian questions about man as a machine with a human soul added to it, perhaps making its will known through the pineal gland just as we can make 'humanness' available to the Monte Carlo robot by rigging the wheel.

The model we had been using seemed wrong – or at least it led us down dead ends where we did not want to travel. What it told us – and it was not trivial – was that shared sensitivities and biases can produce some strikingly social consequences. For one thing, they produce astonishing stability within groups. People act in accordance with their perceptions and their choices, and they reciprocate accordingly. We created a little discussion group of seven members, to discuss 'psychology and life' (they were all undergraduates). And we administered our test four or five times over a term. Some interesting things happened to the dyads or pairs that composed that group. Certain patterns virtually disappeared over time or occurred eventually at levels below chance. Instances of pairs in which each chose the other with neither feeling chosen in return were gone by the end of the term. So too were cases where both felt chosen by the other but did not choose in return. The transactional process seemed to intensify over time. We left it at that and went off to pursue other matters.

But the problem was to return, and it did so, more than a decade later, when I began a series of studies on growth in human infancy and particularly on the development of human language and its precursors. My first brush with it was in studying the development of exchange games in infancy, when I was struck with how quickly and easily a child, once having mastered the manipulation of objects, could enter into 'handing back and forth', handing objects around a circle, exchanging objects for each other. The competence seemed there, as if *ab ovum*; the performance was what needed some smoothing out. Very young children had something clearly in mind about what others had in mind, and organized their actions accordingly. I thought of it as the child achieving mastery of one of the precursors of language use: a sense of mutuality in action.

So too in a second study in which we were interested in how the child came to manage his attention jointly with others – a prerequisite of linguistic reference. We found that by their first birthday children are already adept at following another's line of regard to search for an object that is engaging their partner's attention. That surely requires a sophisticated conception of a partner's mind.

Yet why should we have been surprised? The child has such conceptions 'in mind' in approaching language. Children show virtually no difficulty in mastering pronouns and certain demonstratives, for example, even though these constitute that confusing class of referring expressions called deictic shifters. A deictic shifter is an expression whose meaning one can grasp only through appreciating the interpersonal context in which it is uttered and by whom it is uttered. That is to say, when I use the pronoun *I*, it means me; when my partner uses it, it refers to him. A spatial shifter pair like *here* and *there* poses the same problem: *here* used by me is close to me; *here* used by you is close to you. The shifter ought to be hard to solve for the child, and yet it isn't.

It *ought* to be, that is, if the child were as 'self-centered' as he is initially made out to be by current theories of child development. For our current theories (with notable exceptions carried over from the past, like the views of George Herbert Mead) picture the child as starting his career in infancy and continuing it for some years after, locked in his own perspective, unable to take the perspective of another with whom he is in interaction. And, indeed, there are even experimental 'demonstrations' to prove the point. But *what* point? Surely not that we can take any perspective of anybody in any plight at any time. We would not have been so slow in achieving the Copernican revolution if that were the case, or in understanding that to the Indians North America must have seemed like *their* homeland. To show that a child (or an adult) cannot, for example, figure out what three mountains he sees before him might look like to somebody viewing them from their 'back' sides (to take as our whipping boy one of the classic experiments demonstrating egocentrism), does not mean he cannot take another's perspective into account *in general*.

It is curious, in view of the kinds of considerations I have raised, that psychological theories of development have pictured the young child as so lacking in the skills of transaction. The prevailing view of initial (and slowly waning) egocentrism is, in certain respects, so grossly, almost incongruously wrong and yet so durable, that it deserves to be looked at with care. Then we can get back to the main issue – what it is that readies the child so early for transacting his life with others on the basis of some workable intuitions about Other Minds and, perhaps, about Human Situations as well. The standard view seems to have four principal tenets:

1. *Egocentric perspective.* That initially young children are incapable of taking the perspective of others, have no conception of Other Minds, and must be brought to sociality or allocentrism through development and learning. In its baldest form, this is the doctrine of initial primary process in terms of which even the first perceptions of the child are said to be little more than hallucinatory wish-fulfilments.

2. *Privacy.* That there is some inherently individualistic Self that develops, determined by the universal nature of man, and that it is beyond culture. In some deep sense, this Self is assumed to be ineffable, private. It is socialized, finally, by such processes as identification and internalization: the outer, public world becoming represented in the inner, private one.

3. *Unmediated conceptualism.* That the child's growing knowledge of the world is achieved principally by direct encounters with that world rather than mediated through vicarious encounters with it in interacting and negotiating with others. This is the doctrine of the child going it alone in mastering his knowledge of the world.

4. *Tripartism.* That cognition, affect and action are represented by separate processes that, with time and socialization, come to interact with one another. Or the opposite view: that the three stem from a common process and that, with growth, they differentiate into autonomous systems. In either case,

cognition is the late bloomer, the weak vessel, and is socially blind.

I do not want to argue that these four premises are 'wrong', only that they are arbitrary, partial and deeply rooted in the morality of our own culture. They are true under certain conditions, false under others, and their 'universalization' reflects cultural bias. Their acceptance as universals, moreover, inhibits the development of a workable theory of the nature of social transaction and, indeed, even of the concept of Self. One could argue against the tenet of privacy, for example (inspired by anthropologists), that the distinction between 'private self' and 'public self' is a function of the culture's conventions about when one talks and negotiates the meanings of events and when one keeps silent, and of the ontological status given to that which is kept silent and that which is made public. Cultures and sub-cultures differ in this regard; so even do families.

But let us return now to the main point: to the nature of transaction and the 'executive processes' necessary to effect it, to those transactional selves hinted at in the title of this chapter. Consider in more detail now what the mastery of language entails with respect to these ideas.

Take *syntax* first. We need not pause long over it. The main point that needs making is that the possession of language gives us rules for generating well-formed utterances, whether they depend on the genome, upon experience, or upon some interaction of the two. Syntax provides a highly abstract system for accomplishing communicative functions that are crucial for regulating joint attention and joint action, for creating topics and commenting upon them in a fashion that segments 'reality', for forefronting and imposing perspectives on events, for indicating our stance toward the world to which we refer and toward our interlocutors, for triggering presuppositions, and so on. We may not 'know' all these things about our language in any explicit way (unless we happen to have that special form of consciousness which linguists develop), but what we do know from the earliest entry into language is that others can be counted upon to use the same rules of syntax for forming and for comprehending utterances as we use. It is so pervasive a system of calibration that we take it for granted. It entails not just the formulas of Grice, or of Sperber and Wilson, or of Putnam to which I referred, but the assurance that mind is being used by others as we use it. Syntax indeed entails a particular use of mind, and however much one may argue (as Joseph Greenberg in his way and Noam Chomsky in his have argued) that we cannot even conceive of alternative ways of using our minds, that language expresses our natural 'organs of thought', it is still the case that the joint and mutual use of language gives us a huge step in the direction of understanding other minds. For it is not simply that we all *have* forms of mental organization that are akin, but that we *express* these forms constantly in our transactions with one another. We can count on constant transactional calibration in language, and we have ways of calling for repairs in one another's utterances to assure such calibration. And when we encounter those who do not share the means for this mutual calibration (as with foreigners), we regress, become suspicious, border on the paranoid, shout.

Language is also our principal means of *referring*. In doing so, it uses cues to the context in which utterances are being made and triggers presuppositions that situate the referent. Indeed, reference plays upon the shared presuppositions and shared contexts of speakers. It is to the credit of Gareth Evans that he recognized the profound extent to which referring involves the mapping of speakers' subjective spheres on one another. He reminds us, for example, that even a failed effort to refer is not just a failure, but rather that it is an offer, an invitation to another to search possible contexts with us for a possible referent. In this sense, referring to something with the intent of directing another's attention to it requires even at its simplest some form of negotiation, some hermeneutic process. And it becomes the more so when the referent is not present or accessible to pointing or to some other ostensive maneuver. Achieving joint reference is achieving a kind of solidarity with somebody. The achievement by the child of such 'intersubjective' reference comes so easily, so naturally, that it raises puzzling questions.

The evidence from early pointing (usually achieved before the first birthday) and from the infant's early following of another's line of regard suggests that there must be something preadapted and prelinguistic that aids us in achieving initial linguistic reference. I do not doubt the importance of such a biological assist. But this early assist is so paltry in comparison to the finished achievement of reference that it cannot be the whole of the story. The capacity of the average speaker to handle the subtleties of ellipsis, of anaphora – to know that, in the locution 'Yesterday I saw *a* bird; *the* bird was singing', the shift from indefinite to definite article signals that the same bird is referred to in the second phrase as in the first – is too far removed from its prelinguistic beginnings to be accounted for by them. One has to conclude that the subtle and systematic basis upon which linguistic reference itself rests must reflect a natural organization of mind, one into which we *grow* through experience rather than one we achieve by learning.

If this is the case – and I find it difficult to resist – then human beings must come equipped with the means not only to calibrate the workings of their minds against one another, but to calibrate the worlds in which they live through the subtle means of reference. In effect, then, this is the means whereby we know Other Minds and their possible worlds.

The relation of words or expressions to other words or expressions constitutes, along with reference, the sphere of *meaning*. Because reference rarely achieves the abstract punctiliousness of a 'singular, definite referring expression', it is always subject to *polysemy*, and because there is no limit on the ways in which expressions can relate to one another, meaning is always underdetermined, ambiguous. To 'make sense' in language, as David Olson argued persuasively some years ago, always requires an act of 'disambiguation'. Young children are not expert at such disambiguation, but procedures for effecting it are there from the earliest speech. They negotiate – even at 2 years of age – not only what is being referred to by an expression, but what other expressions the present one relates to. And children's early monologues, reported by Ruth Weir a generation ago and more recently by Katherine Nelson and her colleagues in the New York Language Acquisition Group, all point to a drive to explore and to overcome ambiguities in the meaning of utterances. The young child seems not only to negotiate sense in his exchanges with others but to carry the problems raised by such ambiguities back into the privacy of his own monologues. The realm of meaning, curiously, is not one in which we ever live with total comfort. Perhaps it is this discomfort that drives us finally to construct those larger-scale products of language – drama and science and the disciplines of understanding – where we can construct new forms in which to transact and negotiate this effort after meaning.

To create hypothetical entities and fictions, whether in science or in narrative, requires yet another power of language that, again, is early within reach of the language user. This is the capacity of language to create and stipulate realities of its own, its *constitutiveness*. We create realities by warning, by encouraging, by dubbing with titles, by naming, and by the manner in which words invite us to create 'realities' in the world to correspond with them. Constitutiveness gives an externality and an apparent ontological status to the concepts words embody: for example, the law, gross national product, antimatter, the Renaissance. It is what makes us construct proscenia in our theater and still be tempted to stone the villain. At our most unguarded, we are all Naive Realists who believe not only that *we* know what is 'out there', but also that it is out there for *others* as well. Carol Feldman calls it 'ontic dumping', converting our mental processes into products and endowing them with a reality in some world. The private is rendered public. And thereby, once again, we locate ourselves in a world of shared reality. The constitutiveness of language, as more than one anthropologist has insisted, creates and transmits culture and locates our place in it – a matter to which I turn next.

Language, as we know, consists not only of a locution, of what is actually said, but of an illocutionary force – a conventional means of indicating what is intended by making that locution under those circumstances. These together consti- tute the speech acts of ordinary language, and they might be considered as much the business of the anthropologist as of the linguist. The speech acts taken only as a phenomenon without psychological implications imply that learning how to use language involves both learning the culture and learning how to express intentions in congruence with the culture. This brings us to the question of how we may conceive of 'culture' and in what way it provides means not only for transacting with others but for conceiving of ourselves in such transactions.

It would not be an exaggeration to say that in the last decade there has been a revolution in the definition of human culture. It takes the form of a move away from the strict structuralism that held that culture was a set of interconnected rules from which people derive particular behaviors to fit particular situations, to the idea of culture as implicit and only semiconnected knowledge of the world from which, through negotiation, people arrive at satisfactory ways of acting in given contexts. The anthropologist Clifford Geertz likens the process of acting in a culture to that of interpreting an ambiguous text. Let me quote a paragraph written by one of his students, Michelle Rosaldo:

> In anthropology, I would suggest, the key development . . . is a view of culture . . . wherein meaning is proclaimed a public fact – or better yet, where culture and meaning are described as processes of interpretive apprehension by individuals of symbolic models. These models are both 'of' the world in which we live and 'for' the organization of activities, responses, perceptions and experiences by the conscious self. For present purposes, what is important here is first of all the claim that meaning is a fact of public life, and secondly, that cultural patterns – social facts – provide the template for all human action, growth and understanding. Culture so construed is, furthermore, a matter less of artifacts and propositions, rules, schematic programs, or beliefs, than of associative chains and images that tell what can be reasonably linked up with what; we come to know it through collective stories that suggest the nature of coherence, probability and sense within the actor's world. Culture is, then, always richer than the traits recorded in the ethnographer's accounts because its truth resides not in explicit formulations of the rituals of daily life but in the daily practices of persons who in acting take for granted an account of who they are and how to understand their fellows' moves.

I have already discussed the linguistics, so to speak, by which this is accomplished. What of the 'cultural' side of the picture? *How* we decide to enter into transaction with others linguistically and by what exchanges, how *much* we wish to do so (in contrast to remaining 'detached' or 'silent' or otherwise 'private'), will shape our sense of what constitutes culturally acceptable transactions and our definition of our own scope and possibility in doing so – our 'selfhood'. As Rosaldo reminds us (using the Ilongot people as contrast) our Western concern with 'individuals and with their inner hidden selves may well be features of *our* world of action and belief – itself to be explained and not assumed as the foundation of cross-cultural study'. Indeed, the images and stories that we provide for guidance to speakers with respect to when they may speak and what they may say in what situations may indeed be a first constraint on the nature of selfhood. It may be one of the many reasons why anthropologists (in contrast to psychologists) have always been attentive not only to the content but to the form of the myths and stories they encounter among their 'subjects'.

For stories define the range of canonical characters, the settings in which they operate, the actions that are permissible and comprehensible. And thereby they provide, so to speak, a map of possible roles and of possible worlds in which action, thought and self-definition are permissible (or desirable). As we enter more actively into the life of a culture around us, as Victor Turner remarks, we come increasingly to play parts defined by the 'dramas' of that culture. Indeed, in time the young entrant into the culture comes to define his own intentions and even his own history in terms of the characteristic cultural dramas in which he plays a part – at first family dramas, but later the ones that shape the expanding circle of his activities outside the family.

It can never be the case that there is a 'self' independent of one's cultural–historical existence. It is usually claimed, in classical philosophical texts at least, that Self rises out of our capacity to reflect upon our own acts, by the operation of 'metacognition'. But what is strikingly plain in the promising research on metacognition that has appeared in recent years – work by Ann Brown, by J.R. Hayes, by David Perkins, and others – is that metacognitive activity (self-monitoring and self-correction) is very unevenly distributed, varies according to cultural background, and, perhaps most important, can be taught successfully as a skill. Indeed, the available research on 'linguistic repairs', self-corrections in utterances either to bring one's utterances into line with one's intent or to make them comprehensible to an interlocutor, suggests that an *Anlage* of metacognition is present as early as the eighteenth month of life. How much and in what form it develops will, it seems reasonable to suppose, depend upon the demands of the culture in which one lives – represented by particular others one encounters and by some notion of a 'generalized other' that one forms (in the manner so brilliantly suggested by writers as various and as separated in time as St Augustine in the *Confessions* and George Herbert Mead in *Mind, Self, and Society*).

It would seem a warranted conclusion, then, that our 'smooth' and easy transactions and the regulatory self that executes them, starting as a biological readiness based on a primitive appreciation of other minds, is then reinforced and enriched by the calibrational powers that language bestows, is given a larger-scale map on which to operate by the culture in which transactions take place, and ends by being a reflection of the history of that culture as that history is contained in the culture's images, narratives, and tool kit.

In the light of the foregoing, we would do well to re-examine the tenets of the classical position on egocentrism with which we began:

Egocentric perspective. Michael Scaife and I discovered, as I mentioned in passing, that by the end of the first year of life, normal children habitually follow another's line of regard to see what the other is looking at, and when they can find no target out there, they turn back to the looker to check gaze direction again. At that age the children can perform none of the classic Piagetian tasks indicating that they have passed beyond egocentrism. This finding led me to take very seriously the proposals of both Katherine Nelson and Margaret Donaldson that when the child understands the event structure in which he is operating he is not that different from an adult. He simply does not have as grand a collection of scripts and scenarios and event schemas as adults do. The child's mastery of deictic shifters suggests, moreover, that egocentrism *per se* is not the problem. It is when the child fails to grasp the structure of events that he adopts an egocentric framework. The problem is not with competence but with performance. It is not that the child does not have the capacity to take another's perspective, but rather that he cannot do so without understanding the situation in which he is operating.

Privacy. The notion of the 'private' Self free of cultural definition is part of the stance inherent in our Western conception of Self. The nature of the 'untold' and the 'untellable' and our attitudes toward them are deeply cultural in character. Private impulses are defined as such by the culture. Obviously, the divide between 'private' and 'public' meanings prescribed by a given culture makes a great difference in the way people in that culture view such meanings. In our culture, for example, a good deal of heavy emotional weather is made out of the distinction, and there is (at least among the educated) a push to get the private into the public domain – whether through confession or psychoanalysis. To revert to Rosaldo's Ilongot, the pressures are quite different for them, and so is the divide. How a culture defines privacy plays an enormous part in what people feel private *about* and when and how.

Unmediated conceptualism. In the main, we do not construct a reality solely on the basis of private encounters with exemplars of natural states. Most of our approaches to the world are mediated through negotiation with others. It is this truth that gives such extraordinary force to Vygotsky's theory of the zone of proximal development. We know far too little about learning from vicarious experience, from interaction, from media, even from tutors.

Tripartism. I hope that all of the foregoing underlines the poverty that is bred by making too sharp a distinction between cognition, affect and action, with cognition as the late-blooming stepsister. David Krech used to urge that people 'perfink' – perceive, feel, and think at once. They also *act* within the constraints of what they 'perfink'. We *can* abstract each of these functions from the unified whole, but if we do so too rigidly we lose sight of the fact that it is one of the functions of a culture to keep them related and together in those images, stories and the like by which our experience is given coherence and cultural relevance. The scripts and stories and 'loose associative chains' that Rosaldo spoke of are templates for canonical ways of fusing the three into self-directing patterns – ways of being a Self in transaction.

Finally, I want briefly to relate what I have said in this chapter to discussions of narrative. Insofar as we account for our own actions and for the human events that occur around us principally in terms of narrative, story, drama, it is conceivable that our sensitivity to narrative provides the major link between our own sense of self and our sense of others in the social world around us. The common coin may be provided by the forms of narrative that the culture offers us. Again, life could be said to imitate art.

References

Austin, J., *How To Do Things With Words*. Oxford: Oxford University Press, 1962.

Benveniste, E., *Problems in General Linguistics*. Carol Gables, Fla: University of Miami Press, 1971.

Bruner, J., and Tagiuri, R., 'The perception of people', in G. Lindzey (ed.), *Handbook of Social Psychology*. Reading, Mass.: Addison-Wesley, 1954.

Bruner, J., 'Learning how to do things with words', in J. Bruner and A. Garton (eds), *Human Growth and Development*. Wolfson College Lectures, Oxford: Oxford University Press, 1976.

Chipman, S.F., Segal, J.W., and Glaser, R., *Thinking and Learning Skills*, Volume II. Hillsdale, NJ: Erlbaum, 1985, esp. chs 14, 15 and 17.

Chomsky, N., *Reflections on Language*. London: Temple Smith, 1976.

Clark, E., 'From gesture to word: on the natural history of deixis in language acquisition', in J. Bruner and A. Garton (eds), *Human Growth and Development*. Wolfson College Lectures, Oxford: Oxford University Press, 1976.

Clark, E., 'Awareness of language: some evidence from what children say and do', in A. Sinclair, R.J. Jarvella and W.J.M. Levelt (eds), *The Child's Conception of Language*. Berlin and New York: Springer-Verlag, 1978.

Donaldson, M., *Children's Minds*. New York: Norton, 1978.

Evans, G., *The Varieties of Reference*, ed. J. McDowell. Oxford: Oxford University Press, 1982.

Feldman, C., 'Epistemology and ontology in current psychological theory'. Address to the American Psychological Association, held at Anaheim, California, September 1983.

Geertz, G., *The Interpretation of Cultures*. New York: Basic Books, 1973.

Greenberg, J., *Essays in Linguistics*. Chicago: University of Chicago Press, 1957.

Greenberg, J. (ed.), *Universals of Language*. Cambridge, Mass.: MIT Press, 1963.

Grice, H.P., 'Logic and conversation', in P. Cole and J.L. Morgan (eds), Syntax and Semantics. Volume III: *Speech Acts*. New York: Academic Press, 1975.

Hockett, C., *The View From Language: Selected Essays*. Athens, Ga: University of Georgia Press, 1977.

Jones, E.E., 'Major developments in social psychology during the last five decades', in G. Lindzey and E. Aronson (eds), *Handbook of Social Psychology* (3rd edn), Volume I. New York: Random House, 1985.

Kasermann, M.L., and Foppa, K., 'Some determinants of self-correction: An interactional study of Swiss-German', in Werner Deutsch (ed.), *The Child's Construction of Language*. London: Academic Press, 1981.

Lyons, J., *Semantics*, Volumes I and II. Cambridge: Cambridge University Press, 1977.

Mead, G.H., *Mind, Self, and Society*. Chicago: University of Chicago Press, 1934.

Nelson, K., and Grundel, J., 'At morning it's lunchtime: a scriptal view of children's dialogue'. Paper presented at the Conference on Dialogue, Language Development and Dialectical Research, University of Michigan, December 1977.

Olson, D., 'Language and thought: aspects of a cognitive theory of semantics', *Psychological Review*, 1970, 77, 257–73.

Piaget, J., *The Child's Conception of Space*. London: Routledge & Kegan Paul, 1956.

Putnam, H., *Mind, Language and Reality*, Volume II. Cambridge: Cambridge University Press, 1975.

Rosaldo, M., *Knowledge and Passion*. Stanford: Stanford University Press, 1980.

Rosaldo, M., 'Toward an anthropology of self and feeling', in R. Schweder and R. Le Vine (eds), *Culture Theory: Essays on Mind, Self and Emotion*. Cambridge: Cambridge University Press, 1984.

Scaife, M., and Bruner, J., 'The capacity for joint visual attention in the infant', *Nature*, 1975, 253, 265–6.

Scheler, M., *The Nature of Sympathy*. London: Routledge & Kegan Paul, 1954.

Sperber, D., and Wilson, D., 'Mutual knowledge and relevance in theories of comprehension', in N.V. Smith (ed.), *Mutual Knowledge*. London: Academic Press, 1982.

Taylor, C., 'Dwellers in egocentric space', *The Times Literary Supplement*, 11 March 1983.

Trevarthen, C., 'Instincts for human understanding and for cultural cooperation: their development in infancy', in M. von Cranach, K. Foppa, W. Lepenies and D. Ploog (eds), *Human Ethology: Claims and Limits of a New Discipline*. Cambridge: Cambridge University Press, 1979.

Turner, V., *From Ritual to Theatre*. New York: Theater Arts Press, 1973.

Weir, R., *Language in the Crib*. The Hague: Mouton, 1962.

5

The Origins of Inference *

MARGARET DONALDSON

One of the central characteristics of our minds is that we deal not only in what *is* but in what *must be*. We reason that *if* something is true *then* something else about which we have no immediate evidence must also be true. Much of the time we do this unreflectingly, hardly noticing the leap, and we do it with smooth-running success.

A good deal of our everyday reasoning is of course merely probabilistic – a matter of what is most likely to be the case. The doorbell rings and we say: 'Ah, that must be John. He promised to come round after dinner.' In such a case, though we often use the word 'must', no necessity attaches to the conclusion. If it turns out not to be John after all we are not greatly surprised or puzzled. We do not feel that we have to search for an explanation so as to preserve the very structure of our thought.

But now consider a different sort of case. Suppose we put a pound note in an envelope and we keep it in full view on the table in front of us. Then, though we can no longer see the pound note, we know that it *must* be there. If we were to break the seal and find that the money had gone we would have a real problem on our hands. The problem would be no less than this: we would be forced to doubt our memory or our eyesight or our

*Paper presented at a meeting of the British Association for the Advancement of Science, Salford, 1980.

rationality. Doubting our memory would amount to questioning one premise, namely: 'I put a pound note in the envelope.' Doubting our eyesight would amount to questioning the other premise: 'No one took it out again.' Doubting our rationality would amount to questioning the validity of the conclusion: 'Therefore it is still there.' In such a case we normally choose to question the premises rather than the structure of our reasoning itself. We say: 'I can't have put it in' or 'Someone must have taken it out again.'

Underlying the rationality that we normally do not even think of questioning are certain basic convictions about the nature of the world. Notable among these is the belief that objects continue to exist when we no longer see them – a belief obviously at stake in the example we have just considered and in virtually all our reasoning. But this conviction itself is bound up with something even more fundamental and pervasive – with the knowledge that we live in a universe where the occurrence of one thing may preclude the occurrence of another. It is on this knowledge that we base our beliefs as to the necessity of the conclusions we draw. In other words, deductive inference rests on our understanding of incompatibility. If X is true, then Y cannot also be true. If it is true that I put a pound note in the envelope then it is not at the same time true that I put it in my pocket or in the waste paper basket. How does this fundamental conviction arise in our minds?

There are two questions that need to be distinguished. First of all, what is the source of the *notion* of incompatibility? And second, how do we come to know what precludes what in the real world? It is with the first of these questions that this paper is concerned.

If we confine our thinking on the subject to a consideration of reasoning as it is expressed in verbal propositions, the question seems at first sight hard to answer. Verbal reasoning commonly appears to be about 'states of affairs' – the world seen as static, in a cross-section of time. And considered in this way the universe appears to contain no incompatibility: things just are as they are. That object over there is a tree; that cup is blue; that man is taller than that man. Of course these states of affairs preclude infinitely many others, but how do we come to be aware of this? How does the idea of incompatibility arise in our minds? Certainly not directly from our impressions of things-as-they-are.

But then it is a grave mistake to suppose that in general we get our knowledge of the world in this kind of way. We do not sit around passively waiting for the world to impress its 'reality' on us. Instead, as is now widely recognized, we get much of our most basic knowledge through taking action. And we can scarcely do this to any extent at all without encountering the fact that the taking of one action often precludes the taking of another. If action X is 'realized', then action Y is not. If a child throws a rattle out of the pram she cannot also and at the same time put it in her mouth.

Yet even this does not go far enough, for it still does not make clear how the awareness of incompatibility can arise. An action, like a tree or a cup, just *is*. Thus the only time when awareness of incompatibility is at all likely to arise in the mind is before actions are carried out. And this means that we are talking about a clash of impulses – or intended acts. As soon as a child entertains simultaneously more than one intention, she is in a situation of potential conflict between impulses to action. And, clearly, she has now the opportunity to recognize that they cannot both be realized.

How early in life does this begin to happen? Bruner (1971) has given us relevant evidence in the shape of a detailed and illuminating account of a conflict which undoubtedly occurs very frequently. If a child with a toy in her hands is offered another, she will almost certainly have two impulses: to hold on to the one she already has and to accept the new one. What then happens?

Consider first what happens at the level of observable behaviour. Bruner studied children between 4 months and 17 months of age. Of the 4-month-olds he says:

> Children of this age were, for the most part, unable to deal with more than one object at a time. A second toy would either be ignored or, more probably, would so pre-empt attention that the child would drop the toy in hand as he fastened visually on the new one being presented. The loss of grasp seemed inadvertent, appearing to take place when the child's attention went to the new object.

Bruner also tells us that, until about 7 months, if a child has an object in one hand he does not seem to know how to transfer it to the other. He does not reach across the body's midline, and so if a second object is offered to a hand already full then that hand 'will tense and the infant will bang the new object with a clenched hand holding the original object' (Bruner, 1969). From about this age on, skill in hand-to-hand transfer begins to develop and soon, by means of it, the child comes to be able to accept two objects. The offer of a third, however, when both hands are full, still presents a serious problem.

Progress thereafter consists in learning to put objects into store, generally on the lap or on the arm of the chair. But this in itself often leads to fresh conflict. When the child has put an object in his lap in order to reach for a new one, the sight of the object he has just stored seems to trigger an impulse to pick it up again, which is incompatible with the intention that led him to put it down in the first place, namely the intention to receive the newly presented toy.

By the age of 12 months, however, these conflicts have often been resolved in such a way that a smooth and successful routine is established. The child will now commonly anticipate the offer of the next toy, placing an object in store before the new one is offered so as to have a hand free and ready.

So what must have happened as regards the organization and control of behaviour for this to be possible? Clearly one thing is that the child has learned to inhibit certain impulses in order to be able to realize others. The impulse to pick up the toy that he himself has just laid down is a good example. The 12-month-old child has come to recognize that if he lifts A again, he is not going to be able to accept B. Either A or B in the hand but not both at once: he has to choose.

As so often in talking of the early stages of life, we must remind ourselves that our own talk about these things can have no verbal counterpart in the minds of the children. Clearly they do not say to themselves, at the age of 1 year: 'I have to choose'. But it is evident that by the time these storage routines are well established they do know they have to choose. They have a sense of options – which is to say that they have constructed mental representations of possible future states. The essential prerequisites for inference are thus present. These are, first of all, the experience of having impulses which conflict with one another so that they cannot both be realized; and, second, the possession of a nervous system capable of representing the outcomes of these impulses as options for consideration. Beyond this it is necessary that the representations should not just be momentary. They must endure. They must be retained so that, when one option is chosen, awareness of the other – the rejected one – remains. Awareness of what is *not* actualized is crucial.

How are we to tell when this begins – when the child not only chooses between consciously entertained possibilities but retains and reflects on the rejected alternatives? It seems that clear evidence has to depend on the use of language. It is only when the child begins to talk to us about what is not that we can be sure.

There is a considerable literature on negation in early child language and various distinctions between different kinds of negative have been drawn. Negative expressions may constitute refusal to comply ('No' meaning *I won't*), or, somewhat later, they may deny the truth of statements ('No' meaning *it isn't*). Both of these types express dissent or disagreement. But there are other kinds of negative which have no such functions, but which simply comment on what is not the case. It is the latter which provide the clearest early evidence that reflection on logical possibilities has begun.

First, however, let us look at some evidence about the development of dissenting negatives of the kind that deny propositions. Roy Pea (1980) studied the ability of very young children to judge statements false or true, and managed by skilful techniques to elicit such judgements from children as young as 18 months in some cases, and with increasing frequency from 24 months onwards. His procedure was to say to the child 'Give me the car' (and so on, naming one of a set of objects) and then, when the child had done so, to make a statement about the object, a statement which might be true or false. When the statement was false the children would often correct it, saying 'no' or 'no, it's not'. This finding gives important confirmation to earlier claims based on observations of spontaneous speech at these ages. Pea argues that this kind of negation is crucial in logic and that his results therefore bear on the question of the origins of logical thought, a view with which I would not disagree.

However, I want now to offer for comparison a brief dialogue which took place between myself and Laura, a child aged 2 years 10 months at the time. I had been working with Laura regularly for some months, seeing her two or three times a week. Usually we went downstairs from the nursery to the room where we had our sessions together, but one day this room was not available. As we stood outside the nursery door, I said: 'We're going upstairs today, Laura.' And Laura replied: 'Not going down.' The words and circumstances were noted immediately afterwards. It is significant that the dialogue took place before we had begun to move towards the stair.

Now Laura's words provide a good example of what we may call a 'negative of comment'. She is not disagreeing. Rather she is commenting on what I say, noting what is implied.

There were at the time two incompatible actions open to us. I proposed one. Laura showed by her words that, while accepting this one, she *entertained the possibility of the other*. The occurrence of the words 'no' and 'not' in this kind of quiet reflective remark is likely to be the earliest unambiguous evidence we get that a rejected alternative is being consciously held in a child's mind.

It is easy to give logical form to the dialogue between Laura and myself.

First premise (implicit): A or B but not both.
Second premise (explicit): A.
Conclusion (explicit): Therefore not B.

But are we really to say that Laura is reasoning in this kind of way? The case for answering in the affirmative would look stronger if Laura had not expected to be taken downstairs. Given that she did, it may seem more sensible to say that she is merely marking a difference, a departure from normality. After all, if she was given her milk in a white cup when she was used to having a blue one she might say: 'Not blue' and there would be no inference in that. However, in one important respect this would not be a strict analogue. The conversation outside the nursery door took place while we were standing still, before we had begun to move upstairs. Thus the child is reflecting on

what is not yet actual but only projected. Clearly this streng-
thens the case for supposing her to be genuinely aware that *if* A,
then not B – or in other words: 'We're going up, *so* we're not
going down'.

It is also worth noting that if there had been no departure
from normality, no expectation involved, there would have
been no point, humanly speaking, in Laura's comment. It
would not have been the kind of thing that people of any age
are given to saying to one another. So the pragmatic, interpersonal function of her words was certainly that of marking the
exceptional nature of what was about to happen; but this does
not by itself have any bearing on the presence or absence of
inference.

It may help towards a better appreciation of the issues if we
consider the following verbally stated problem: 'If you are in a
place where you can either go up or down and you go up, then
what follows?' It is virtually certain that Laura would not have
been able to deal with this problem, even though the solution is
directly supplied by her own spontaneous comment. So why
not? Is it merely that the language would be too difficult for her?

There can be no doubt that the wording of this question
would be beyond the comprehension of a 2-year-old, but that is
not all. More important, more fundamental than any difficulty
with specific words or constructions, is the contrast between
thinking about a situation which you are actually in and being
called on to think about that same situation when you are
remote from it in space and time. It is one thing to be standing
outside a doorway, expecting to go somewhere and feeling
surprise or interest in a change of plan, eager to let someone
know that you are aware of the change. It is another thing
entirely to be asked to consider this situation when you are not
in it, when you have no feelings about it and when there is
absolutely nothing that you want to say.

In the first case, thinking is wholly embedded in a context of
action, direct perception, purpose and feeling. It arises spontaneously within this context. It does not come as a response to
a question posed 'out of the blue' by someone else. To think in
the first fully embedded way one need not deliberately turn – or
set – one's mind.

By contrast, any problem about a remote setting calls for

thought that is disembedded in some degree. However, a further distinction must be drawn between thinking which arises directly out of one's own life's concerns, even though it is not about the immediate present, and thinking which is called for by a problem set by someone else. In the former case, the thinking is still embedded in the life of the mind – in a setting of memories, hopes and purposes – if not in the life of the senses and the muscles. But when some other person asks us to consider a problem unconnected with anything that we have been doing, or are planning to do, or that spontaneously engages our minds, then a new, big step in the direction of disembedding is called for.

This would be the case with the verbal problem about going up and down stairs if it were suddenly shot at Laura when she had been doing something else entirely – playing, for instance, in the nursery. The problem, simple as it is, would be set apart, encapsulated, extrinsic to her concerns. And so it would make cognitive demands of certain very special kinds.

It is important to try to understand the nature of these demands since the development of the mind – certainly the development of the educated mind in our kind of culture – consists in no small measure in coming to be able to meet them. (For a more extensive discussion see Donaldson, 1978.)

The difficulties which disembedded problems present do not reduce to questions of linguistic *knowledge*. Yet they have a great deal to do with the handling of language all the same.

When such a problem is presented words are generally used. The problem is posed verbally, even if there is also a non-verbal component in the shape of objects to consider or manipulate. Now the point is that in our ordinary embedded thinking and language-using we do not normally even attempt to make sense of words in isolation. We interpret what people say with the help of what they do – their gestures, their movements – and with the help of the entire setting within which the speech occurs. We use all the clues we can get to arrive at what the speaker means. But when we are given a disembedded problem we have the task of figuring out what the words mean: the words on their own. This is an austere and difficult enterprise for the human mind. It might be supposed that interpreting language is merely a matter of knowing word meanings and putting these together having regard to the rules of grammar; but this is not how we habitually proceed (c.f. Johnson-Laird, 1983). In important respects it is alien to us to take the spare, bare words and hold to them alone. Instead, as much research has now shown, we make various kinds of 'cognitive contribution', often without noticing what we are doing – that is, without awareness of what we ourselves bring to the meaning that we derive.

There is a story – a true story – about a robot called Freddy which illustrates the point well. Freddy was once given the task of putting all the objects on a table into a big box. The operation ran smoothly and successfully until the very end, but then Freddy did something that no human being would ever do. He tried to put the box in the box. Or, if that is to speak too humanly, he picked the box up and put it down again, and picked it up and put it down again – and presumably would have gone on doing so indefinitely. He had been instructed to put 'all the objects on the table' into the box and, after all, the box was one of the objects on the table.

Human beings, however, have a powerful urge that was lacking in Freddy. They have an urge to make sense of what they hear – or read. So in this case they would add to the instruction, without even noticing what they were doing, the crucial phrase 'except the box itself'. Then the instruction 'makes sense' in relation to the world we know and to purposes we can understand, and all seems well.

The cognitive contributions that we bring to the interpretation of language may be of many different kinds and we may make them with more or less ease and immediacy. Bransford and his colleagues (see, for instance, Bransford and McCarrell, 1975) have provided interesting evidence of what happens in a situation where the sense-making contributions are hard to provide. Consider one of their examples, the sentence: 'The haystack was important because the cloth ripped'. The words are familiar, the construction is straightforward but we do not feel that the utterance as a whole makes sense. Sudden illumination comes with the information that it is 'about' a parachute descent.

Yet it is by no means the case that without this information the sentence is meaningless. On its own, it conveys a limited amount of perfectly good meaning. It tells us that a piece of cloth became torn and that this event caused a haystack to acquire importance. However, we are not satisfied to accept just this much information and no more. We try instead to construct a setting in which such a causal link could reasonably arise, in which these words might reasonably have been spoken; and we have difficulty in doing so because an uncommon setting is required, one that does not readily come to mind.

By contrast, of course, if the same words were physically embedded, we would have no such effort to make. The setting would be provided. It would be all around us, we would be *in* it. If two people had just made a parachute descent together and one of them said to the other after landing: 'The haystack was important because the cloth ripped' (a statement that would admittedly seem a bit unemotional in these circumstances) then a feeling of full comprehension would be immediate. There would be no special cognitive work to do in order for sense to be made.

With this in mind, let us return to the difference between Laura's recognition that going up entails not going down when she is faced with these real options, and the ability to make 'the same' inference in dealing with a disembedded problem. It should now be clear how far the one is from the other.

At first, in their very beginnings, language and thought are entirely embedded in the here and now of personal activity and interaction. This is 'present moment embedding'. The next step comes with extension into the past and into the future, but still the focus is on the personal life – plans, memories, hopes and fears. We may speak now of 'own-life embedding'. Beyond this again, progress lies in the growth of the ability to think and talk about things that are not only further off in space and time but remote from the thrust of one's own concerns.

It is on this kind of development – though not of course on this alone – that the achievements of logic, mathematics and science depend. These achievements, however, are hard won. They call for a kind of mental discipline and self-control which never comes easily to us. We do not readily relinquish the support for thought which an embedding context provides.

Thus it is hard for us to deal in meaningless symbols – Xs and Ys, Ps and Qs. But it is a mistake to suppose that expressing a problem in meaningful words rather than abstract symbols necessarily reduces the likelihood of error. For the meaningful words may merely tempt us, rousing in us the old familiar sense-making urge. And what 'making sense' often amounts to – as the work of Bransford and his colleagues shows – is an activity that may be called 'imaginative embedding' by means of which we contrive to slot the problem in to some setting with which we are familiar, in which we feel we know the rules. If the setting that we provide is appropriate to the problem then all goes well. But if the setting is inappropriate – and especially if, without noticing, we alter the problem slightly to make it fit – then at once we are in trouble.

Thus it is entirely to be expected that what appears in its formal structure as 'the same' reasoning problem should prove to be of very different difficulty when it appears under different guises. And we should not underestimate how hard an achievement strict disembedded reasoning is for the human mind.

References

Bransford, J.D., and McCarrell, N.S., 'A sketch of a cognitive approach to comprehension: some thoughts about understanding what it means to comprehend', in W.B. Weimer and D.S. Palermo (eds), *Cognition and the Symbolic Processes*. Hillsdale, NJ: Erlbaum, 1975.

Bruner, J.S., 'Eye, hand and mind', in D. Elkind and J.H. Flavell (eds), *Studies in Cognitive Development: Essays in Honour of Jean Piaget*. Oxford: Oxford University Press, 1969.

Bruner, J.S., 'The growth and structure of skill', in K.J. Connolly (ed.), *Motor Skills in Infancy*. New York: Academic Press, 1971.

Donaldson, M., *Children's Minds*. London: Fontana/Croom Helm, 1978.

Johnson-Laird, P.N., *Mental Models*. Cambridge: Cambridge University Press, 1983.

Pea, R.D., 'Logic in early child language', *Annals of the New York Academy of Sciences*, 1980, 345, 27–43.

6
The early emergence of planning skills in children

JUDY S. DELOACHE

and ANN L. BROWN

Very young children have always been somewhat mysterious to their parents: The common term, the 'terrible twos', in part reflects parents' lack of understanding of the manifold changes taking place in their offspring. Very young children have also remained mysterious to scientists, in large part because they have been, until recently, relatively neglected by developmental researchers.

Several years ago, we (Brown and DeLoache, 1978) and others (e.g. Gelman, 1978) decried the lack of knowledge of early development. We made the point that most of what was known about very young children was negative – a great deal was known about what they didn't know and couldn't do, but little about areas in which they might be knowledgeable and competent.

There were several factors that had contributed to the scientific neglect of this age group. For one thing, neither of the dominant developmental theories provided much impetus to study young children. The original learning theories held that the same basic principles of conditioning and reinforcement could account for behavioral change at all phylogenetic and ontogenetic levels; hence, there was no reason to look for uniqueness among young children. And the most influential theorist of cognitive development, Jean Piaget, treated early childhood (post-infancy) as a period of relative cognitive quiescence with little major developmental change of interest going on.

In addition, many of the favourite topics of developmental researchers were believed to be inapplicable to very young subjects. For example, mnemonic strategy development was one of the most extensively researched topics in the 1970s, but very little research was directed to children younger than 5, because they were assumed (with some evidence) to be incapable of strategic effort. The question of whether the tasks and methods used with other subjects were really appropriate for young children was not seriously considered.

Another impediment to research on early cognitive development was purely practical – young children are notoriously uncooperative subjects (DeLoache, 1980); it is hard to figure out how to elicit and sustain their interest and enthusiastic participation. Fortunately, this last hurdle has been systematically surmounted. Researchers interested in early development have become increasingly ingenious in their methods, and, as a consequence, young children have come to be seen as increasingly ingenious themselves.

The recognition of the necessity of designing experimental tasks that map appropriately onto young children's existing abilities and proclivities has led to the development of experimental procedures specifically adapted to this age group. One important aspect of these procedures is the attempt to avoid confounding content with process. Virtually any subject of any age can display more sophisticated cognition when reasoning about familiar than unfamiliar matters. Since very young children are universal novices (that is, they are relatively unfamiliar with any given domain; Brown and DeLoache, 1978), it is especially important that researchers interested in underlying processes tailor their tasks to their subjects' current knowledge. As a result of efforts to do this, research with very young children has flourished in recent years, and much positive information has accumulated about early development.

In fact, the literature now abounds with examples of the competence of the very young child (so much so that there have been recent calls for us not to overestimate early competence just as we had previously underestimated it – Flavell, 1982;

Gelman, 1983). However, most of this literature involves abilities that are domain- or age-specific; that is, the competence that has been uncovered usually has to do with a particular domain of knowledge or with a particular age group.

Our interests, and the focus of this chapter, concern more general aspects of early cognition, those aspects that do not set young children apart as unique, but rather those that are the same or similar over age. We will pursue two interrelated themes here: (1) the active and *self-initiated* nature of young children's cognition and learning and (2) the *self-directed* nature of their cognitive efforts.

Through a selective review of some recent research on early cognition, we will seek to demonstrate that young children's learning and problem-solving is more a matter of active experimentation than passive observation. We will also examine the extent to which their activities are governed by the same or similar processes of self-regulation characteristic of older children and adults. These are the processes by which people regulate their cognition and action, such as planning ahead, monitoring progress, evaluating success, correcting errors and so forth. We have argued that these general cognitive processes are important across a wide variety of situations throughout the life span (Brown and DeLoache, 1978). Our current interest is in the earliest manifestations of these general skills. To what extent do very young children exhibit the cognitive strategies that older individuals use to regulate their cognition? In what ways do early strategies resemble their more mature counterparts, and in what ways do they differ?

To summarize, the broad themes of this chapter will be the following:

1. The young child is an active enquirer, not a passive observer, of his or her world.

2. The child's enquiry is methodical and, to a greater or lesser extent, self-regulated; it is not random or externally determined.

3. The young child's methods of enquiry are in many important ways similar to those of older children and adults.

4. The young child's methods of enquiry are in many important ways different from those of older children and adults.

In other words, we assume continuity over age in the processes and mechanisms of learning, and we wish to identify the precursors or potential precursors of later skills.

Self-initiated learning

A good starting point for our discussion is to take note of the fact that children learn in situations where there is no external pressure to improve or change, no obvious guidance, and no feedback other than their own satisfaction. In a very real sense they act as little scientists, creating theories-in-action (Karmiloff-Smith, 1979a, 1979b, 1984) that they challenge, extend, and modify on their own volition. Children are not only problem solvers, but also problem creators: they not only attempt to solve problems presented to them, but they also seek novel challenges. The adult struggling to solve a crossword puzzle has much in common with the young child trying to fit together a set of nesting cups.

Some of the best evidence of self-motivated and self-directed learning comes from situations in which children spontaneously operate on a problem with no external pressure or instruction. We will give some examples of learning of this kind, pointing out commonalities across children of disparate ages when faced with appropriate tasks.

Our initial illustration comes from 18- to 42-month-old children engaged in free play with a set of nesting cups (DeLoache, Sugarman and Brown, 1985). Five cups were dumped on the table in front of each child, and the experimenter simply said, 'These are for you to play with.' Although the children had previously seen the cups nested together, there was no real need for them to attempt to nest the cups themselves; they could easily have done something else with them. However, almost all the children immediately started trying to fit the cups together, often working long and hard in the process.

The children from all age groups in the study behaved similarly in that they spontaneously adopted the goal of nesting the cups together and then engaged in extensive goal-directed activity. They also monitored the success of their actions (which is quite obvious in the case of nesting cups – either the cups fit together or they do not), and they attempted to correct their own errors.

Not surprisingly, the older children were more successful than the younger ones at achieving a fully nested or seriated set of cups. However, the different age groups did not differ in total amount of activity with the cups, nor in the likelihood that an error would be followed by a correction attempt. The most interesting age differences that occurred had to do with the children's procedures for improving their performance, in particular their strategies for correcting the errors they made in combining cups.

The most primitive strategy, more prevalent among the young children, was *brute force*. When a larger cup was placed on a smaller one, the children would press down hard on the non-fitting cup, trying to force it to fit into the one below. Rather than question her original action and change something about the selection or ordering of the cups, the child seemed to assume that greater physical effort might solve the problem.

A second strategy that was somewhat more characteristic of the younger than the older children was to attempt a *local correction*. After putting two non-fitting cups together, the child removed the top cup and then did one of two things: she either looked for an alternative base for the non-fitting top cup, or she tried an alternative top on the original base. Both of these ploys involved minimal restructuring and required considering only one relation (between two cups) at any one time. A third characteristic action of the younger children was to respond to a cup that would not fit into a partially completed set of cups by *dismantling the set*. Not infrequently, this involved taking apart not just the incorrectly sequenced cups, but also properly nested ones.

When the older children (30- to 42-month-olds) were faced with non-fitting cups, they often engaged in more advanced correction strategies, strategies that involved *consideration of the whole set* of cups. With these more sophisticated strategies, the children simultaneously considered multiple relations among the set of cups. In one, *insertion*, the children took apart a stack of cups just to the point that enabled them to insert a new cup into its correct position. In the other late-developing strategy, *reversal*, the child would, immediately after placing two non-fitting cups together, reverse the relation between them.

The importance of considering multiple relations in making corrections is illustrated by cases where a young child had correctly nested all but one cup, but then lacked effective strategies for combining the last cup with the rest. Consider a child who had nested cups 1 through 4 (3 nested in 4, 2 in 3 and 1 in 2), but then tried to place cup 5 (the largest cup) on top of the nest. The child pressed and twisted the non-fitting cup repeatedly, but when this brute force approach failed, dismantled the whole stack and started again. A reversal of cup 5 and the nest (1–4) would have immediately solved the problem, but reversal was not in this child's repertoire. Similarly, a young child who had assembled cups 1, 2, 4 and 5 had no reliable means of inserting cup 3 into the nest and so took them all apart and began again.

In their spontaneous manipulations of a set of nesting cups, very young children thus progress from trying to correct their error by (a) exerting physical force without changing any of the relations among the elements, to (b) making limited changes in a part of the problem set, to (c) considering and operating on the problem as a whole. This sequence may represent a general acquisition sequence in children's learning, for a very similar progression is also seen in other problem domains.

We take as an example 4- to 7-year-old children attempting to construct a railway circuit for a toy train (M.J. Kane and A.L. Brown, work in progress; Karmiloff-Smith, 1979b). The child is shown cardboard sections of track that, if joined together correctly, will make a continuous circuit for the train. After seeing a very simple track completed, the child is given a more complex version that involves combining both straight and curved segments (see Figure 6.1). One solution is to alternate the straight and curved pieces (resulting in a roughly rectangular construction – b), and another is to put together curved pieces to form arches at both the top and bottom and then join each arch with straight pieces (a somewhat oval-shaped track results – a).

Many of the youngest children began by placing randomly selected pieces next to each other and hence ended up in a position that could not possibly lead to a solution (Figure 6.1, c and d). Of interest is what the children did next. Even the

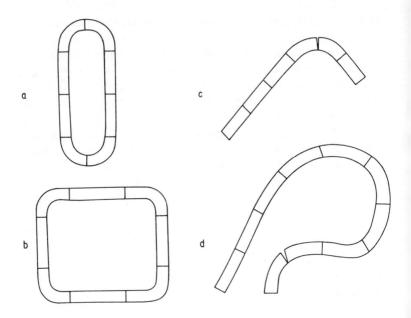

Figure 6.1
Source: Karmiloff-Smith 1979b

youngest persisted in their efforts, but their strategies changed with age and experience in a way quite analogous to the stacking-cups task described above.

The first line of attack was the *brute force* approach; the children tried to make the tracks fit by firmly pushing them together to close up gaps. Just as the younger children with the nesting cups sometimes repeatedly pressed and twisted the same set of cups, these children were sometimes extremely persistent in attempting to physically 'shape up' their construc- tions. One 5-year-old girl, for example, spent several minutes tidying her circuit, pushing and pulling the various segments without changing their relative positions. As soon as she managed to get one bit tidied up, another part would pop out of place, and she would address herself to it.

The next stage was *local correction*: the child would remove the last piece and try to fix it, ignoring the rest of the construction that might be equally in need of work. The third stage was one where the child, seeing that she was in trouble, *disassembled the entire construction* and started again, even though part of the construction could be salvaged.

Just as with the nesting cups, the more mature response to the railway-track task involved viewing the *construction as a whole*. This enabled the children to rearrange those pieces that needed rearranging, while leaving correct sections intact. Often the corrections would involve the strategic *reversal* of already joined pieces or the *insertion* of a critical straight (or curved) piece between two joined pieces.

This developmental progression was seen both across ages (macrogenetic change) and within an age group (microgenetic change) when children were given a long time to work on the problem (Karmiloff-Smith, 1979b). It was also seen when the level of problem difficulty was controlled by giving all children the same partially completed constructions to repair. The children were asked to recognize and fix up disasters supposedly created by other children (M.J. Kane and A.L. Brown, in progress).

The nesting cups and the train-track tasks thus reveal common features of young children's problem-solving. In both cases, young children spontaneously monitored the success of their own goal-directed efforts and attempted to correct their errors. Their strategies for error correction showed a similar progression with age, from (a) a purely physical solution (force) directed towards a single, misplaced element, to (b) a consideration of the relation between the non-fitting element and another, to (c) a consideration of the entire problem set and the internal relations among the elements within it.

One thing to note about this progression is that it is not simply a domain-specific or an age-related sequence. The same sequence of correction strategies appeared in the two different tasks even though the range of ages differed – 18- to 42-month-olds in the nesting-cups task and 4- to 7-year-olds in the train task. However, the nesting cups represented a challenging but manageable task for the younger children, and the train track did the same for the older ones. Thus, the sequence appears to represent a general acquisition mechanism that underlies learning to solve a variety of different problems.

The correction strategies just described provide clear examples of spontaneous improvement in young children's problem-solving methods. However, the exercise of these strategies is driven by the presence of error, the absence of success. The active nature of young children's learning and problem-solving is reflected especially clearly in examples in which children work toward improvement even in the face of success. In the railway track studies, some children actually dismantled a perfectly workable system and built a new one, pointing out that there were several solutions to the problem (M.J. Kane and A.L. Brown, work in progress).

As a final and more extensive example of children's self-generated improvement, consider a group of 4- to 7-year-olds playing with a set of trick wooden blocks (Karmiloff-Smith and Inhelder, 1974/5). The children were asked to balance rectangular wooden blocks on an narrow metal rod fixed to a larger piece of wood (Figure 6.2). Standard blocks had their weight evenly distributed, so the solution was to balance them at the geometric center. The trick blocks had the weight of one side varied either conspicuously (by glueing a large square block to one end of the standard rectangular block) or inconspicuously (by inserting a hidden weight into a cavity on one end of the rectangular block).

At first, the children made the blocks balance by *brute trial and error* using proprioceptive information to guide action. Their behavior was directed purely at the goal of balancing; and they were successful, even with the trick blocks. However, the children did not rest with their initial, practical, success but, quite without external pressure, set about trying to uncover the rules governing the balancing of these particular blocks. In other words, even though the children had succeeded completely at the task set for them – balancing the blocks – they went on to try to figure out and test an explanation for what they had observed.

Their initial theories typically involved incomplete rules that produced some successes, but also some errors. A common early theory developed by the children was to concentrate exclusively on the length of the blocks and attempt to balance all blocks at their geometric center. This worked for the standard unweighted blocks, but not for either kind of weighted blocks. Since the weighted blocks did not conform to the theory, they were discarded as exceptions – 'impossible to balance' – even

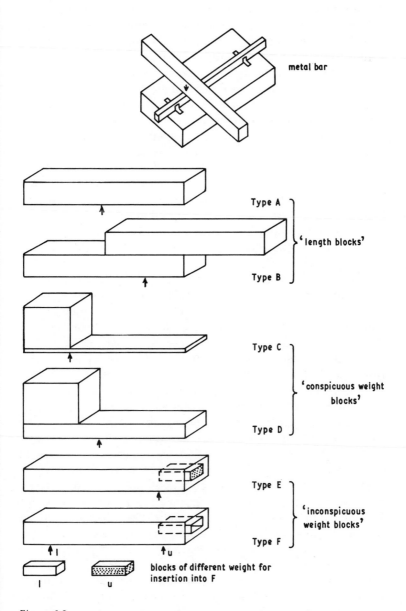

metal bar

Type A ⎤
         ⎬ 'length blocks'
Type B ⎦

Type C ⎤
         ⎬ 'conspicuous weight blocks'
Type D ⎦

Type E ⎤
         ⎬ 'inconspicuous weight blocks'
Type F ⎦

l   u   blocks of different weight for insertion into F

Figure 6.2
Source: Karmiloff-Smith and Inhelder, 1974/5

though the child had previously been able to balance them all.

After this theory was well established and was working well for balancing the unweighted blocks, the child became discomforted by the number of, and regularity of, the impossible-to-balance set. A new theory that covered the conspicuous weight blocks was then developed and juxtaposed with the initial theory. The children now took into account the conspicuous weight that was visible on one end of those blocks and adjusted the point of balance accordingly. Inconspicuous weight problems still generated errors; they looked identical to the unweighted blocks and were, therefore, subjected to the dominant geometric center rule. When they did not behave according to the theory, they were discarded as 'impossible-to-balance' anomalies. The children's verbal responses reflected these juxtaposed solutions, with length justifications given for unweighted blocks and weight justifications given for conspicuously weighted blocks.

After establishing and practicing the juxtaposed theory, the young theorists were made increasingly uncomfortable by the remaining exceptions to their own rules, and a reorganization was induced that resulted in a single rule for all blocks. The children now paused before attempting to balance any block and roughly assessed the point of balance. Their verbal responses reflected consideration of both length and weight: 'You have to be careful, sometimes it's just as heavy on each side and so the middle is right, and sometimes it's heavier on one side.' Only after inferring the probable point of balance did the child place the block on the bar.

The main point about all of these examples is, *why does the child bother*? Implicit in the situations is the goal of nesting the cups, completing the railway circuit, or balancing the blocks; however, the child is free to terminate her efforts at any point. But she persists. She persists even in the face of frustration; she persists for long periods of time; and she persists even when an adequate solution has been reached. She not only corrects errors, she improves upon successes. Reorganization and improvement in procedures is not solely a response to failure; it often occurs when the child has adequately functioning procedures but seeks to improve them. Here, it is not failure that directs the change but success, success that the child wishes to refine and extend (Karmiloff-Smith, 1984).

The progression from theories that fail to theories that work can be explained in terms of goal-directed learning – the child wishes to correct errors and achieve her goal. But the pressure of work on adequate partial theories to produce more encompassing theories is very similar to what occurs in scientific reasoning. Like the scientists, it is essential that the child first gain control of simple theories in her quest for a more complex and more encompassing theory. Karmiloff-Smith and Inhelder refer to this as *creative simplification*.

The construction of false theories or the overgeneralization of limited ones are in effect productive processes. Overgeneralization, a sometimes derogatory term, can be looked upon as the *creative simplification* of a problem by ignoring some of the complicating factors (such as weight in the block study). This is implicit in the young child's behavior but could be intentional in the scientist's. Overgeneralization is not just a means to simplify but also to unify; it is then not surprising that the child and the scientist often refuse counterexamples since they complicate the unification process. However, to be capable of unifying positive examples implies that one is equally capable of attempting to find a unifying principle to cover counterexamples, and hence modify the theory (Karmiloff-Smith and Inhelder, 1974/5, p. 209).

Progress comes only when the more restricted partial theory is well established and the learner is free to attempt to extend the theory to other phenomena. In this way the theorists, be they children or scientists, are able to discover new properties that in turn make it possible for new theories to be constructed (Carey, 1985).

The studies reviewed in this section make it clear that, faced with problems to solve, where they are interested in the outcome and understand the goal, even 2-year-olds actively and systematically pursue the solution. The metaphor of the child as a little scientist seems an appropriate description of the active way in which the child explores her environment, tests theories in action, and modifies her approach to problems as a result of experience. This is not to claim that the 2-year-old possesses strategic abilities comparable to the adult, or even the 8-year-old. Nor is it to claim that the theory-building of the preschooler is comparable to the forms of scientific reasoning that are perfected during adolescence and adulthood. But certainly the precursors of active and systematic problem-setting and problem-solving emerge early in the child's life.

Self-direction of learning

In the previous section, we attempted to illustrate the active and self-*initiated* nature of young children's learning and problem-solving. In this section we will consider the self-*direction* or self-*regulation* of cognition, and the data we will discuss necessitate a reassessment of many long-standing views of very young children's cognitive capabilities.

Deliberate remembering. As was mentioned in the introduction to this chapter, young children have generally been considered incapable of planful or strategic learning. This is not to say that young children were thought to be unable to learn, only that they could not actively and deliberately regulate their own learning opportunities and experiences.

In the large body of research on memory development, there was considerable negative evidence, that is, evidence that young children failed to behave strategically in a variety of experiments (Brown, 1975; Flavell, 1970; Kail and Hagen, 1977). Consider the following imaginary, but prototypical, memory experiment. Two groups of children – 4-year-olds and 8-year-olds – are told that they should remember a list of words that is then read to them. Between the items and during the delay interval following the presentation of the words, the older children are observed actively rehearsing the words, whispering them over and over to themselves. The 4-year-olds give no evidence of rehearsal of any sort. On the recall test, the 8-year-olds' performance is vastly superior to that of the younger subjects. One inference drawn by the investigators is that the age difference in memory performance is in part due to the difference in strategic effort.

This imaginary study, and many real ones like it in the literature, provides us with clear, positive information about the older participants. We know that they are capable of spontaneous strategic effort in the service of remembering, and we are left with the hypothesis (easily confirmed in subsequent research) that such strategic intervention facilitates learning and remembering the material.

What does the study tell us about the younger subjects – the 4-year-olds who don't rehearse and don't remember very well? We only know that in this particular situation they did not spontaneously apply strategic effort to help themselves remember and that their memory performance was quite poor. What are we to infer from this negative evidence? That 4-year-olds do not adopt memory goals and are incapable of strategic effort? As we have already said, that is indeed the inference that was commonly drawn. Little consideration was given to the possibility that the memory task used might be inappropriate in numerous ways for tapping any mnemonic competence that 4-year-olds might possess.

But now, consider a different, non-imaginary memory experiment with young children. Wellman, Ritter and Flavell (1975) had 3- and 4-year-old children watch while a small toy dog was hidden under one of three cups, and the children were instructed to remember where the dog was. The children were anything but passive as they waited alone during the delay interval. Presumably to avoid forgetting the correct location, they often stared fixedly at the correct hiding place, refusing to be distracted, until they were permitted to retrieve the dog. Some children displayed various behaviors that resemble well-known mnemonic strategies, including clear attempts at *retrieval practice* (such as looking at the target cup and nodding yes, looking at the non-target cups and nodding no) and *retrieval cueing* (such as marking the correct cup by resting their hand on it or moving it to a salient position). These efforts were rewarded; children who prepared actively for retrieval in these ways more often remembered the location of the hidden dog.

This study and others (cf. Istomina, 1975) called into question the assumption that preschool children were incapable of deliberate remembering and wholly non-strategic. It also provided clues as to what early memory strategies might look like.

Even earlier evidence of planning for future retrieval has been found (DeLoache, Cassidy and Brown, 1985). Children between 18 and 24 months of age were observed playing a memory ('hide-and-seek') game: an attractive toy (Big Bird) was hidden in a variety of natural locations in a laboratory playroom, such as behind a pillow on a couch or under a chair. The child was instructed that, 'Big Bird is going to hide, and when the bell rings, you can find him.' A timer was set to indicate the delay interval (3–4 minutes), and when the bell rang, the child was allowed to retrieve the toy. During the delay interval, the child was engaged by the experimenter in play and conversation. Of interest is what happened in this interval when the child was not required to be involved in the memory task.

Just like the older children in the Wellman, Ritter and Flavell (1975) study, these young subjects did not passively wait during the interval. Instead, they often interrupted their play, engaging in a variety of activities that indicated they were still preoccupied with the memory task. The children frequently talked about the toy (saying, for example, 'Big Bird'), the fact that it was hidden ('Big Bird hiding'), where it was hidden ('Big Bird chair'), or about their plan to retrieve it later ('Me find Big Bird'). Other rehearsal-like behaviors included looking or pointing at the hiding place, hovering near it, and attempting to peek at the toy. Although less systematic and well-formed than an older person's sophisticated rehearsal strategies, the young child's precautions similarly function to keep alive the information to be remembered, that is, to remind the child of the hidden toy and its location.

It is notable that these young children did not engage in these ingenious 'keep-alive' activities when the toy was visible during the retention interval. For example, in one condition, the child was told that 'Big Bird needs to take a nap now, and when the bell rings, you can go and get him up.' The toy was then placed so that it remained visible (instead of hiding it under a cushion, the experimenter might place it on top of the cushion). Under these conditions, the children ignored the toy. They also ignored the toy if the experimenter was charged with the responsibility for retrieving it. When the experimenter announced at the beginning of the trial 'Big Bird is going to hide, and when the bell rings, *I'll* find him', the children did not concern themselves with the toy during the interval.

When there was something to remember and when the burden of remembering fell on them, 22-month-old children thus prepared themselves for future retrieval. These preparations are by no means identical to the full-blown retrieval activities employed by adults, but they share many features with them and qualify as early precursors of active memory strategies (DeLoache, 1984, 1985). At the very least, data such as these make us pause before diagnosing young children as passive learners, for the hallmark of these descriptions is the self-directed, inventive, active intervention on the part of the child (DeLoache, 1985; DeLoache and Brown, 1979).

The above series of imaginary and real studies demonstrates the absolutely crucial importance of having age-appropriate tasks. Whether or not preschool children can adopt a goal of remembering and organize their behaviour in accordance with that goal depends on whether the memory task maps onto their existing abilities and proclivities. Young children will search for an object hidden in the environment well before they will search for information stored in their minds (Brown and DeLoache, 1978; Wellman and Somerville, 1982). They enjoy hiding and finding games; they play them spontaneously. It is precisely in this sort of situation that they are mnemonically competent; they understand the imperative to remember and they are capable of doing things to help themselves do so.

Cognitive skills are not all-or-none phenomena. The child who is hopelessly inept in one situation (rehearsing a list of words so as to recall them later) may appear skilled in a different form of the same basic problem (keeping track of where an object is hidden so as to retrieve it later). If we wish to understand the development of sophisticated cognitive skills, we cannot ignore their earlier, more primitive precursors. We must look at different age groups, including very young children, and we must be prepared to look at them through superficially different tasks, but tasks that are carefully selected to tap the same underlying processes.

Searching intelligently

The memory studies described above are not isolated examples of the early emergence of active 'strategy-like' behaviour in very young children, and one area that is replete with examples of early competence is search. In both diary studies of infants'

memory-related behavior in the home (Ashmead and Perlmutter, 1980) and laboratory investigations with age-
appropriate tasks (Sophian, 1984), there are many examples of
persistent and intelligently regulated search by children below
2 years of age.

We will now discuss a set of studies of searching by children
ranging from infants to 4-year-olds; the tasks are superficially
dissimilar, but in all of them the child's searching is based on
an inference drawn from a sequence of remembered events, an
inference about where a missing object *must* be. To be
successful in these tasks, the child must draw an intelligent
inference about the whereabouts of the missing object and then
organize her search accordingly.

First, let us consider inferential searching in 3- and 4-year-old
children who have already developed this skill to a level of
some sophistication. Preschoolers were taken on a trip around a
set of locations on their school playground (Haake, Somerville
and Wellman, 1980). They carried a camera in a bag and took it
out of the bag to take photos at the first three locations at which
they stopped. The camera remained out of sight and was not
mentioned again until a later stop (the seventh out of eight
places), at which point it was 'discovered' by the wily
experimenter to be missing. At the end of their circuit, the
children were asked to find the missing camera. Based on the
children's experience with the camera, it must be in a critical
search space defined by the point at which it was last seen
(location 3) and the point at which it was discovered to be
missing (location 7); it could not, logically, be at locations 1, 2, 7
or 8.

Children as young as 3½ years showed significant logical
searching on this task: they not only went first to a location
within the critical area (usually location 3 – the last place they
had seen the camera), but they also restricted their searching to
within the critical area (3–6). The 3-year-olds in this research
thus used their memory for where they had experienced an
object to infer where the now-missing object must be. The
children used their own cognition as the basis for organizing or
regulating their subsequent actions.

Intelligent memory-based searching has also been reported
for younger children in the hide-and-seek task described

above. In a variation of the basic delayed retrieval task, DeLoache and Brown (1984) confronted 18- to 30-month-old children with a violation of their expectancy about the location of the hidden toy: the experimenter hid the toy as usual, but then she surreptitiously moved it without the child's knowing.

Even the youngest children searched very persistently on their surprise trials, when they were in fact at the correct location. A good example of highly persistent searching is the surprise trial behavior of a 23-month-old boy: he looked under the couch cushion where his toy had been hidden, then pulled the cushion completely off the couch and examined the area, turned around to say 'No?' to his mother, and then turned back and briefly checked the correct hiding place again.

What was especially interesting was the subsequent search patterns. The older (24- to 30-month-old), but not the younger (18- to 23-month-old), children engaged in intelligent searching. Failing to find their toy at the expected location, they tended to search places that would be plausible locations if their memory for its hiding place were essentially correct. The majority of their additional searches were at locations that were in some way related to the correct location. For example, if the toy had been hidden under a couch pillow before the experimenter secretly moved it, the child might search under an adjacent couch pillow or behind or beneath the couch. The younger children simply tended to search for the missing toy in places where it had been hidden previously (a very common type of error in memory for location and object permanence tasks: Harris, 1975). Thus the older but not the younger children systematically organized their search for a mysteriously missing object based on an inference drawn from their remembered experience with the object.

The types of locations searched gave some clues as to the nature of the inferences drawn. In some cases, the children seemed to infer that they must have misremembered some detail about the toy's location, such as which particular one of a category of locations it was. An example would be the child's searching under a different pillow after failing to find the toy under the pillow it had been hidden with. Sometimes the older subjects seemed to infer that an intervening event was responsible for the unexpected absence of the toy. One child, for example, looked in the desk drawer in which his toy had been hidden and queried 'Did Mickey Mouse fall out?' Similarly, on their second surprise trial, some subjects inferred (correctly) that the experimenter had once again moved their toy. A 29-month-old girl whirled around from her search of the correct (but empty) location and yelled to the experimenter 'Jackie, *you* took him.'

Finally, consider a very simple inferential search task used by Somerville and Haake (1983) with still younger subjects, 9- to 18-month-old infants. The infants were shown a small desirable object in the experimenter's hand. The hand was then closed around the object and passed under the first of two covers on a table. In between the covers, the experimenter opened her hand to show the child either that the object was still present in her hand or that it was missing. The experimenter then proceeded to pass her hand under the second cover, and immediately thereafter showed the child her open, empty hand. The event in between the two covers, in which the experimenter demons-trated that she did or did not still hold the object, defined a critical search space. An infant who draws the correct inference from the event should search under the appropriate cover for the object. Children as young as 15 months usually did search the correct location, showing that they were capable of inferring from the sequence of events where the object had to be.

Examples such as these illustrate the importance of selecting a search task that maps on to the child's current abilities. In many search studies, older but not younger children search approp-riately, and developmental differences are most apparent when one considers the systematicity of search patterns (DeLoache, 1984; Sophian, 1984; Wellman and Somerville, 1982). But, obviously, younger and older are relative terms. The efficient older children (27 months) in the DeLoache and Brown study would be the inefficient younger sample in the playground search studies of Haake, Somerville and Wellman (1980). Similarly, DeLoache and Brown's inefficient younger subjects (21 months) were older than the competent infants observed by Somerville and Haake.

There is no denying that search skills develop with age; older children have a greater variety of systematic search skills that can be applied more widely. At the same time, however, we should not overlook the fact that even infants, when faced with goals they understand, draw intelligent inferences concerning the probable place of missing objects. The tendency to search intelligently is present very early in life, and experience provides the opportunity for the child to expand and refine these skills.

Primitive versus sophisticated competence

In the preceding sections, we have emphasized the self-initiated and self-directed nature of young children's cognition. We have highlighted many similarities in the cognitive activity of young children and older individuals. In particular, we have tried to make the point that many self-regulatory skills are present in the behaviour of very young children. However, early competence does not imply that there is nothing left to learn. Impressed as we may be by young children's ingenuity, we should not forget that they still experience a great deal of difficulty harnessing their natural proclivities as active learners to external demands – for example, to the forms of learning required in schools.

The search skills reviewed earlier provide a case in point. Notwithstanding the preschooler's precocity in searching for lost objects in simple environments, the skill continues to develop slowly (Drozdall and Flavell, 1975). Preschool searchers have problems when they must survey the contents, not of the external world, but of their own minds, in order to retrieve information from memory (Brown and DeLoache, 1978). Searching logically and exhaustively through a target category of remembered words is not a routine occurrence until the late grades (Kobasigawa, 1977); and selectively searching one's retention of even more complex materials such as expository texts can be problematic even for high-school and college students (Brown and Campione, 1978; Brown, Smiley and Lawton, 1978; Kobasigawa, Ransom and Holland, 1980). All of these tasks require that the learner define the logical search set and search exhaustively within it, but it is a long way from 3-year-olds' ability to find a lost camera in their playground (Haake, Somerville and Wellman, 1980) to the ability to retrieve relevant material in one's mind when taking an examination

(Brown, Smiley and Lawton, 1978).

Our interest in very young children stems in part from a desire to achieve a more complete account of development than has often been the case. We doubt that there are many, if any, areas in which development consists of a leap from the complete absence of a skill to its full-blown presence. Generally, the longer and more closely we look, the more intermediate steps we see. Given gradual development from simple, primitive procedures to more complex, comprehensive skills, how do we go about identifying these early forms? How do you know a precursor when you see one?

The search for precursors is inherently tricky. One must chart a course between the Scylla of ignoring early abilities that are related to later ones but that differ from them in many ways and the Charybdis of mistakenly accepting as precursors skills that are superficially similar but are actually unrelated to the mature ability in question. On the other hand, we cannot expect a precursor to be a mini-version of the later skill; it will by definition have some different characteristics, perhaps fulfill slightly different functions, be limited to somewhat different domains and so forth. On the other hand, we must also be cautious in deciding that the abilities demonstrated by the young child are early forms of those present in the older individual. In the past, the field of developmental psychology was not well served by ignoring the competencies possessed by very young children. The future of our discipline will be served no better by exaggerating their competence.

References

Ashmead, D.H., and Perlmutter, M., 'Infant memory in everyday life', in M. Perlmutter (ed.), *New Directions in Child Development*, No. 10: *Children's Memory*. San Francisco: Jossey-Bass, 1980.

Belmont, J.M., and Butterfield, E.C., 'Learning strategies as determinants of memory performance', *Cognitive Psychology*, 1971, 2, 411–20.

Brown, A.L., 'The development of memory: knowing, knowing about knowing, and knowing how to know', in H.W. Reese (ed.), *Advances in Child Development and Behaviour*, Volume X. New York: Academic Press, 1975.

Brown, A.L., and Campione, J.C., 'Permissible inferences from cognitive training studies in developmental research', in W.S. Hall and M. Cole (eds), *Quarterly Newsletter of the Institute for Comparative Human Behaviour*, 1978, 2, 460–53.

Brown, A.L., and DeLoache, J.S., 'Skills, plans and self-regulation', in R. Siegler (ed.), *Children's Thinking: What Develops?* Hillsdale, NJ: Erlbaum, 1978.

Brown, A.L., Smiley, S.S., and Lawton, S.C., 'The effects of experience on the solution of suitable retrieval cues for studying texts', *Child Development*, 1978, 49, 829–35.

Carey, S., *Conceptual Change in Childhood.* Cambridge, MA: MIT Press, 1985.

DeLoache, J.S., 'Naturalistic studies of memory for object location in very young children', in M. Perlmutter (ed.), *New Directions for Child Development: Children's Memory*, No. 10. San Francisco: Jossey-Bass, 1980.

DeLoache, J.S., 'Oh where, oh where: memory-based searching by very young children', in C. Sophian (ed.), *Origins of Cognitive Skills.* Hillsdale, NJ: Erlbaum, 1984.

DeLoache, J.S., 'Memory-based searching in very young children', in H. Wellman (ed.), *The Development of Search Ability.* Hillsdale, NJ: Erlbaum, 1985, pp. 151–83.

DeLoache, J.S., and Brown, A.L., 'Looking for Big Bird: studies of memory in very young children', *Quarterly Newsletter of the Laboratory of Comparative Human Cognition*, 1979, 53–7.

DeLoache, J.S., and Brown, A.L., 'Intelligent searching by very young children', *Developmental Psychology*, 1984, 20, 37–44.

DeLoache, J.S., Cassidy, D.J., and Brown, A.L., 'Precursors of mnemonic strategies in very young children's memory for the location of hidden objects', *Child Development*, 1985, 56, 125–37.

DeLoache, J.S., Sugarman, S., and Brown, A.L., 'The development of error correction strategies in young children's manipulative play,' *Child Development*, 1985, 56, 928–39.

Drozdall, J.G., and Flavell, J.H., 'A developmental study of logical search behaviour', *Child Development*, 1975, 46, 389–93.

Flavell, J.H., 'Developmental studies of mediated memory', in H.W. Reese and L.P. Lipsitt (eds), *Advances in Child Development and Behaviour*, Volume V. New York: Academic Press, 1970.

Flavell, J.H., 'On cognitive development', *Child Development*, 1982, 53, 1–10.

Gelman, R., 'Cognitive development', *Annual Review of Psychology*, 1978, 29, 297–332.

Gelman, R., 'Recent trends in cognitive development', in J. Schierer

130 *Making Sense*

and A. Rogers (eds), *The G. Stanley Hall Lecture Series*, Volume III. Washington, DC: American Psychological Association, 1983.

Haake, R., Somerville, S.C., and Wellman, H.M., 'Logical ability of young children in searching a large-scale environment', *Child Development*, 1980, 51, 1299–1302.

Harris, P.L., 'Development of search and object permanence during infancy', *Psychological Bulletin*, 1975, 82, 332–44.

Istomina, Z.M., 'The development of voluntary memory in preschool-age children', *Soviet Psychology*, 1975, 13, 5-64.

Kail, R.V., Jr, and Hagen, J.W. (eds), *Perspectives on the Development of Memory and Cognition*. Hillsdale, NJ: Erlbaum, 1977.

Karmiloff-Smith, A., 'Micro- and macro-developmental changes in language acquisition and other representational systems', *Cognitive Science*, 1979a, 3, 91–118.

Karmiloff-Smith, A., 'Problem solving construction and representations of closed railway circuits', *Archives of Psychology*, 1979b, 47, 37–59.

Karmiloff-Smith, A., 'Children's problem solving', in M. Lamb, A.L. Brown and B. Rogoff (eds), *Advances in Developmental Psychology*, Volume III. Hillsdale, NJ: Erlbaum, 1984, 39–90.

Karmiloff-Smith, A., and Inhelder, B., 'If you want to get ahead, get a theory', *Cognition*, 1974/5, 3, 195–212.

Kobasigawa, A.K., 'Retrieval strategies in the development of memory', in R.V. Kail, Jr, and J.W. Hagen (eds), *Perspectives on the Development of Memory and Cognition*. Hillsdale, NJ: Erlbaum, 1977.

Kobasigawa, A.K., Ransom, C.C., and Holland, C.J., 'Children's knowledge about skimming', *Alberta Journal of Educational Research*, 1980, 26, 169–82.

Ornstein, P.A., and Naus, M.J., 'Rehearsal processes in children's memory', in P.A. Ornstein (ed.), *Memory Development in Children*. Hillsdale, NJ: Earlbaum, 1978.

Somerville, S.C., and Haake, R.J., 'Selective search skills of infants and young children'. Paper presented at the Biennial Meeting of the Society for Research in Child Development, Detroit, April 1983.

Sophian, C., 'Developing search skills in infancy and early childhood', in C. Sophian (ed.), *Origins of Cognitive Skills*. Hillsdale, NJ: Erlbaum, 1984.

Wellman, H.M., Ritter, R., and Flavell, J.H., 'Deliberate memory behaviour in the delayed reactions of very young children', *Developmental Psychology*, 1975, 11, 780–7.

Wellman, H.M., and Somerville, S.C., 'The development of human search ability', in M.E. Lamb and A.L. Brown (eds), *Advances in Developmental Psychology*, Volume II. Hillsdale, NJ: Erlbaum, 1982.

7

Thought from language: the linguistic construction of cognitive representations

CAROL FLEISHER FELDMAN

Let me begin by distinguishing between two aspects of each and every cognitive task, whether it be a judgment of equality in a conservation task, the solving of the mathematics story problem, responding as a partner in a conversational dyad or interpreting a story. The first aspect is the by now familiar operational component of the task. Once the subject is shown the beakers or told about the price and number of apples, something must be *done* about them, some mental action undertaken. We know now that the nature and quality of these mental acts varies more or less systematically with age, with problem domain, with context or setting. Mental acts are the means whereby we come to *know* about the world; and so I will call them collectively the *epistemic* aspect of cognition.

But all such epistemic acts involve a second aspect. For mental acts act on inputs, which have, first, to be *construed*. And so, before the judgment of equality of water in two differently shaped beakers can be made, the subject must first construe or represent mentally the state of affairs of the water in the beakers. It is this construal of the situation by the problem solver – *his* image or description – that he operates on: *his* not ours, not a physicist's, and not, certainly, an aboriginal, uninterpreted world that simply is as it is. When we operate epistemically on an input, we also create or construe a reality. That is, the subject must construct a state of affairs that, for the purposes of the epistemic task at hand, is to be taken as given. This too is a mental process, and it is as inescapably present in every cognitive task as its epistemic aspect. The construction and stipulation of representations of reality is the *ontic* aspect of cognition and it is different from the epistemic.

Cognitive development is concerned with the growth of mental life in the child. But cognitive development as a field was shaped largely in the terms set by Jean Piaget (1977). He was mainly attentive to the growth of the means of knowing – epistemic operations or procedures for interpreting events in the world. In broad brushstrokes, he told us in these terms about how the *general* characteristics of reasoning changed with development. But in the small details, Piaget and others observed many irregularities in and many deviations from the global pattern. One rash conclusion that can be drawn from these irregularities is that there is *no* general shape to reasoning at different ages. Another is that the form of the 'reality' being reasoned *about* makes as great a difference as the epistemic operations used at different ages, that variations in ontic or 'reality'-constructing processes are as crucial as changes in operations. Many cognitive developmentalists, adopting this latter view, have revised various Piagetian procedures by manipulating variations in materials, instructions or context in the hope of accounting for deviations from predictions based on developmental level or age alone. The implicit notion of development that lies behind such studies is that *both* age *and* context or content matter. But even when both are varied, the *systematic* affects seem to be attributable to age; context or content seem somewhat unpredictable in their effects even when their effect is considerable. We seem to have no general theory to account for variations in performance produced by content or context. Is it the case, then, that content or context, the ontic side of knowing, is not amenable to systematic theoretical description of the kind Piaget offered for genetic epistemology? Does the ontic side of things – how tasks are represented – require another kind of theory?

Considering his emphasis on the operations of knowing, Piaget was right to call his enterprise genetic epistemology. Of course all operations of knowing apply to something (content) under some circumstances (context): all events are constituted of content and context. With respect to the psychological status of those events in the world, Piaget had little to say. His official response to questions about how reality should be construed in the context of genetic epistemology was to say that he was a naive realist. Naive realism is a philosophical position concerning reality that says that what exists in the world is no different from the world as it appears in everyday life. Piaget hoped, by invoking naive realism, to bypass all issues of metaphysics. But in the context of his theory of genetic epistemology, such a claim was genuinely problematic. Indeed, the present crisis of confidence in general claims about age-related cognitive change may have this problem at its root. For as I shall discuss presently, objects of knowledge do not have invariant form across levels of development. Their representation also changes with age and development. If naive realism describes anyone's ontology, it cannot be that of the young child. And Piaget himself must have known this. If the mental operations (epistemological procedures) of pre-adolescence (concrete operations) operate only on *objects*, while the mental operations of adolescence (formal operations) operate only on *propositions*, then the change from one of the other is not just a matter of epistemological operations but also a matter of how 'reality' is re-encoded from objects to propositional form. It is not just the operations that change, but the things on which they operate.

Whether or not Piaget was right in his description of the systems of thought at different ages, or right to suggest that his descriptions actually were known in some way by children (Feldman and Toulmin, 1976), he was surely right to suggest that thinking at different ages was susceptible to being described systematically. What is wrong is to think that we can make a coherent systematic description of age-related epistemological change without an accompanying description of the nature of the mental representation of reality reasoned about by those processes.[1]

1 A theory of the nature of the world is an ontological theory, and a description of the child's systematic reconstrual of the world could be considered a description of genetic ontology. It is the other face of the cognitive domain. What is the nature of the things that are thought about and how are

But naive realism won't work even in adult cognition. Before the subject can make a judgement about the materials presented to him he must first make a mental representation of the situation. It is this *mental representation* that he thinks about when he undertakes the experimenter's task. And where does it come from; who shall be given credit for the representation? Shall we say that the person (at any age) merely copies external reality, has copies passively stamped into his mind by the environment? No serious psychologist would accept such a view. It is now taken for granted that representations are always encodings in some system – be it mathematics, language, images. The properties of the coding system contribute to the patterning of the representation. And usually, a number of coding systems are available among which to choose a medium of representation. So if the subject is not a passive copier of the aboriginal reality, in one way or another he *constructs* his representations of the world.

This constructivist view of mental representations has been particularly well explicated by Nelson Goodman (1984), the philosopher. In his *Ways of Worldmaking*, Goodman says: 'the overwhelming case against perception without conception, the pure given, absolute immediacy, the innocent eye, substance as substrate, has been so fully and frequently set forth – by Berkeley, Kant, Cassirer, Gombrich, Bruner and many others as to need no restatement here'. Goodman enumerates some of the procedures we use in constructing worlds: we compose and decompose for varying purposes, we weight and emphasize features differently, we impose order, we delete and supplement. So mental representations are constructed and the question is, how and from what? Goodman gives a philosopher's answer: from versions that were themselves earlier constructions.

For Goodman, and for many others who want to account for

---

they reasoned about? To say this may seem to beg the question. Once we give Piaget up can we now get the simplifying stipulation of naive realism back? If we are willing to forego systematic developmental description, can we not forego an ontological theory as well? The answer is that we cannot – not because it is a foregone conclusion that there is systematic change on the ontological side in development (but, see Bruner *et al.*, 1966), but because naive realism won't work even in adult cognition.

the human ability to construct representations, the essential tool of construction is language. For him, language as a general purpose symbolic tool creates versions of the world. In doing so it both formulates and objectifies a constituted reality. Through its power to encode and clarify one stipulated version rather than another, it has the power to entrench one version rather than another. In addition, since language embodies conventional cultural categories, it can impose culturally shared (and shareable) meanings on its constructions. For Berger and Luckmann (1966), for example, language – its lexicon and syntax – is the bearer of cultural categories into which the world is divided. So for them reality is socially constructed; that is, it is constructed by each individual anew by the use of a tool that carries with it the social or conventional knowledge of his culture. Of course, people often construct idiosyncratic concepts – perhaps because they are too innocent of the matter to know the conventional categories, perhaps because they are so expert that they reject them. The procedures for these idiosyncratic constructions is less well understood, and less often studied. But they too may involve language, perhaps a more personal language of thinking than the social language of discourse (see Feldman, 1977). All aspects of language – semantics, syntax and pragmatics – must be engaged in the construction: semantics to give a recognizable shape to experience, syntax to place the constitutents of experience into orderly and recoverable structures, pragmatics to permit us to mark our stipulations as the given rather than the new in sentences, and as the topics rather than the comments of our discourse with others.

The ontic aspect of knowing is determined *relative* to epistemic operations. Many different codings of any input situation are possible. We create the particular encodings that we do with an eye to the task at hand. Bickhard and Richie (1983), for example, say that encodings are representations of the world with respect to interpretive devices. The same linkage exists in development generally. Carey (1983), for example, says: 'Developmental psychologists of all persuasions agree on one fact – children's theoretical knowledge is different from that of adults. Children's ontological commitments should differ correspondingly' (p. 17). Ontic structure and status is thus always a stipulation, by which I mean that it is one of many possible ways of construing a situation that is *taken as given* for the epistemic purposes at hand.

Moreover, ontic stipulations are sometimes derived from epistemic operations. One obvious source of ontic structures is one's own prior epistemic operations. Consider an example. The neophyte who does his first few algebra problems by applying a rule that says he can exchange the places of two terms with one another, first A for B and then B for A, uses the rule of commutativity as an epistemological procedure. But soon enough, commutativity will lose its step-by-step procedural quality and become a concept. Exemplars of the commutation concept will be noticed everywhere, and commutation itself will become a concept suitable for reasoning *about*. How, the child might ask, is commutation like or unlike associativity? Now commutation serves as an input to thoughts and operations about *it*. It has moved from an epistemic process into an ontic stipulation, has been 'dumped' into the child's potential store of things that *are*. The existence of the Middle Ages and of primes to infinity are both processes turned into products. Indeed, so even is conservation itself. I want to call this process whereby epistemic operations and their output are given ontological status *ontic dumping*.

This brings us to a striking parallel between language and cognitive structure as we have been discussing it – cognitive structure as a repertory of operations that can be performed on inputs whose constructed pattern is taken as given, though they may be the products of prior constructions. One defining characteristic of all human language, indeed the *essential* defining characteristic according to many of this century's greatest linguists – Roman Jakobson (1981) and the Prague School (Steiner, 1982) among them – is the contrast between the *given* and the *new*. Every language marks this important distinction in its own conventional manner, for without it discourse would be impossible. A first, and surely necessary, condition for successful dialogue is that the topic (the given) be maintained both by and across speakers. Interlocutors can say almost anything they like so long as it is about the topic; the one thing they cannot do is to talk about just any component of the preceding utterance without reference to the topic. To do so gives talk a chain complex quality that makes it appear to move laterally or higgledy-piggledy rather than to progress. The same consequences would follow for thinking undertaken in the form of language. For in order that thinking move forward in a progressive way, it too must maintain a clear marking of the cognitively given (ontically stipulated) and the cognitively new (or epistemic). What is important to keep in mind is that there is nothing *essentially* different about information that appears in the topics and the comments of utterances. What varies is how they are to be *treated*. The very same material that appears on one occasion in a comment as new as new may, for some other purpose, be treated stipulatively in the topic as old; and vice versa. This is a crucial switching operation in both thought and language. To summarize, then, both systems – language and cognition – mark a distinction between information that is to be taken for granted and information that is new and to be further operated upon.

A second parallel between cognition and language follows from the fact that they share this particular patterned duality. It is this: that just as the objects of cognition can be constructed from procedures so the topics of discourse can be constructed from comments. The possibility of transforming the epistemic into the ontic, or ontic dumping, is, then, analogous to the marking of information that was formerly new as something that is now to be treated as old. It has its parallel in the uses of language. When information that has appeared repeatedly in environments where it is marked as a comment is subsequently treated as a topic – that is, is taken for granted in order to comment on it – we can understand that process as the linguistic parallel to ontic dumping.

That the two systems – language and thinking – mark the same duality of old and new may be a purposeful and adaptive convergence, or it may reflect some deeper, structural third factor such as the organization of mind itself, or it may be the merest accident. But whatever its origin, it makes possible the most extraordinarily facilitative relationship between the two systems, language and thought. If comments can be used to construct topics by the use of language, and if these linguistically constructed topics can then be taken as cognitive objects to be reasoned *about*, then comments can be used to construct the stipulative objects of reasoning. This gives the given/new pattern in language a special and definite role in thinking, as one pattern that gives structure to a world of objects that have first to be constructed before they can be reasoned about. And it would follow that linguistic expression would have a specific role as a means for discovering the cognitive representations a speaker has in mind. For it would follow that an examination of dialogue would permit us to see topics being constructed from comments, and, at the same time, we would be watching objects being built.

The capacity to construct representations can be seen by looking at dialogues for newly created topics and for steps along the way to the construction of topics. In the dialogues of adults, one can see the epistemic being converted into the ontic, as earlier–occurring comments are turned subsequently into topics. The patterned procedures for turning comments into topics in adult discourse provide some notion of the full range of possible patterns that can help us in understanding the more limited range of procedures found in the speech of young children. I want to turn first to some examples from adult discourse and then to show how they illuminate the patterns found in the speech of a 2-year-old child, patterns that illustrate preliminary steps along the way to true ontic dumping. These preliminary procedures are, I believe, essential for thinking with language, essential if the two systems, language and thinking, are to be properly tuned to one another.

Consider now the dialogic patterns of graduate students being interviewed about their school experience. In these interviews, one sees the following kinds of topic/comment organization occurring:

(a) *topic innovation*, where a topic is made up of new material;
(b) *comment elaboration*, where new comments in successive utterances are applied to the same old topic;
(c) *comment topicalization*, where matter that previously oc-curred in a comment is first treated as a topic;
(d) *dump topicalization*, where a topic is a reconstruction of material from prior comments into a new, more abstract topic.

The data were interviews about graduate-school experience, with the interviewer interspersing the question 'What?' at random places in the interview. We were interested particularly in how subjects reframed their formulations and remarks. 'What?' is a useful question here because while the interviewer appears to maintain the dialogue, she contributes nothing material to the discourse. In this way, we could observe the subject's elaboration of his own topic without the intrusion of material from the interlocutor.

The interviewer establishes the first topic:

E: Like I told you before, I want you to tell me your thoughts concerning school.
S: Immediately so many negative aspects flood to mind, but there must be some positive aspects that keep me here.

Comment elaboration: *positive and negative aspects* are new comments introduced on the old topic.

E: What?
S: Well, right off the bat I can think of two positive things about graduation school: what you get at the end of it and what you get during it: hopefully you will receive a degree at the end that will allow you to pursue career goals, and while I'm in graduate school there is great potential knowledge that I can pursue.

Comment topicalization: here the comment *positive aspects* is pushed down into the topic and two new comments about it introduced: new *knowledge* now and a *degree at the end*.

S: It's a long process and at each crossroad it seems as though you run into another obstacle or task to overcome. You must stay on top of your grades so you can take prelims and then prelims are another story.

Comment topicalization: the topic now is negative aspects, one earlier introduced in the comment and functioning here anaphorically as topic. The comments on negative aspects are the length and difficulty of the process.

E: What?
S: The prelims are an extremely hard obstacle to bypass. And

only then they allow you to write your dissertation. It seems as if it's an endless process. I guess you have to take one step at a time so that it doesn't become overwhelming.

The topic is still 'negative aspects' and we've now been told about 'endlessness' as well as 'obstacles'.

The next utterance is the first example of dump topicalization – a summary of the full set of comments, reconstrued, as a topic: infantilization.

S: The place is extremely infantilizing. You are constantly pushed to do things and do them well but there is no one there to help you.

Now S goes back to the original topic and generates a new comment through comment elaboration:

S: Education has always been extremely important to me.

If the ability to construct new topics is a standard adult accomplishment, it is not so for young children. Children do not know all of the rules for distinguishing and marking topic and comment in their language when they utter their first words, nor do they seem fully to understand topic maintenance as necessary to discourse. But, in general, some minimal form of topic maintenance, at least, comes very early in language acquisition.

I want now to turn to the speech of a 2-year old child, Emmy, who was taped in dialogue with her parents before going to bed and in monologue alone afterward.[2] Let me briefly contrast the modes of organization seen in the adult discourse above with what is seen in Emmy's speech. Emmy does a good deal of topic innovation. Topic elaboration – adding new comments to old topics – seems to be the next order of business after that and it does not come easily, as we shall see. Emmy is very limited in her ability to topicalize a former comment. And one searches in vain at this age for examples of dump topicalization. Emmy also shows one form of organization rarely found in adults: topic

2   This is an interesting and unusual data set collected by Katherine Nelson and collectively analysed by a group of us including Nelson, Jerome Bruner, John Dore, Julie Gerheart, Dan Stern and Rita Watson.

repetition with an old topic repeated either with its already stated comment, or with no comment at all.

At age 2, Emmy is largely caught up in replaying her parents' old topics and comments. Here is a monologue where she goes back over some material her father produced in an immediately preceding dialogue:

> Oh they at Tanta's do. Big kids like Emmy and Carl and Lise don't cry. They big kids. They sleep like big kids. The baby cries at Tanta's . . . baby can cry, but big kids like Emmy don't cry. They go sleep but the babies cry. The big kids like Emmy don't cry, the big kids haven't cried, but big kids don't cry.

Compare this with what her father had said some minutes before:

> You know Carl doesn't cry, hon. . . . Now remember what I said. Carl doesn't cry and Caitlin and Nick don't cry. You know who cries when they go to bed? Stephen cries, cause Stephen's a little baby. The big kids like you and Nick and Caitlin and Carl. They don't cry, they just go to sleep.

Emmy is also able to introduce topics new to the discourse. In the following excerpt, at the same age, Emmy introduces the new topics: *Carl* and *alligators*. But notice that she makes no comment on them and they are not taken up in discourse.

Fa: You have a good night, honey.
Em: Carl going ring around the rosy.
Fa: Yes. Now he's going night-night. I'll bet Carl's going to sleep too.
Em: Alligators.
Mo: No alligators. You're just silly about that now.
Fa: Good-night, honey, I love you.
Em: Night-night.

But occasionally Emmy *is* able to join a comment to a topic as well. Here is an example of comment elaboration that occurs in the monologue. The topic (cornbread) is one that occurred earlier in dialogue with her parents – her mother informed us later that Emmy loved the bread and ate a lot of it before her parents rationed her.

Daddy make some cornbread for Emmy. Daddy didn't make
that cornbread but then Emmy eat. Da make. Not that bread
for corn Emmy. That bread not for Emmy. Emmy like
cornbread and toast. I don't like milk, apples. I like toast,
muffins, food I like and modens too. I don't like anything
'cept for that bread Daddy has. I don't like the bread
something, Daddy don't like.

The elaborative effort in the comment is crude, to be sure, but
she plainly is trying to hold onto the topic while commenting
on it – though she slips off now and then, as with milk and
apples.

A second example of comment elaboration occurs in dialogue
and is actually about a topic (foot) that Emmy herself introduces. Of her foot, she says that it is *stuck* and that she *has to
take it out.*

Fa: Should Daddy go or should Daddy put a blanket on you?
Em: Put blanket or go out.
Fa: Yeah. What do you want me to do?
Em: My foot stuck.
Fa: It is stuck isn't it?
Em: Take.
Fa: Shall we fix it? Now did you get your foot stuck deliberate-
ly? You're just full of little mischief, aren't you?
Em: I, I have, I have to, take.
Fa: Okay, put you're head down here. I'll put a blanket on you.
Em: I gotta take my foot out.
Fa: Your foot's okay. You can take it out. I know you can take it,
too. I know its not really stuck, is it? No it's not. See?

We can even see the effort at comment elaboration in situations
where Emmy cannot properly lexicalize the topic. From a very
young age, it is evident to her that she must be able to use a
socially shared name as topic if she is going to be able to talk
about it. When her lexicon is deficient she has procedures for
marking a nominal, place-holders, that are an ingenious form of
topic specification possible with a limited vocabulary: in this
case, the expression (for 'intercom'), 'something for the baby,
plug in and say "ahh"'.

I went to sleep and Daddy says buy diapers for Stephen and

Emmy and buy something for Stephen, plug in and say "ahh" on Saturday or some like diaper for Emmy and diaper for baby and then buy something for the something for the baby plug in.

As already noted, we very seldom see comment topicalization at this age, but when it does occur, it seems to follow from prior practice with comment elaboration. Here is one such example:

Fa: and when you wake up we're going to Carl's but you have to go to sleep now. You're such a good girl, pookey.
Em: I sleeping on my bunny.

Here 'bunny' is a new comment on her father's old topic 'sleeping', an example of comment elaboration; and, as we will see, it leads eventually to comment topicalization.

Fa: That's Okay.
Em: I don't want sleep on my.
Fa: Oh, I know you don't want to sleep on your bunny. No. Okay.
Em: (trying to topicalize the former comment *bunny*). The *bad* bunny.
Fa: Okay. Have a good nap, hon. I love you.
Em: The bad . . .
Fa exits, closing door.

If topicalizing a comment is rare at this age, then true dumping is non-existent. It may require more experience with the simpler processes of comment topicalization and comment elaboration, or it may also need to await maturation of the general capacity for abstraction. In any case, it is not within reach of this linguistically precocious girl at 2 years.

In another data set, working with David Kalmar, I have been looking at the way in which epistemic procedures lead to a restructuring of concepts and to the eventual elevation of these procedures to an ontic status. An adult is asked to 'develop' a new concept from successively presented material with which he is, at the start, very unfamiliar. The task is to decide which poems should will be published in a magazine (or which paintings should be shown at an exhibit) and then to formulate an editorial (or curatorial) policy that accounts for the poems (or paintings) selected. The subject is given a series of eight poems (or abstract paintings) and told he will be asked after each poem (painting): 'First, we will ask whether you accept or reject this piece. We will then ask you how you perceive it: that is, what things you notice about it. Then I will ask you to completely describe what your current policy is. Then how this piece affected your policy and how your policy affected your perception of it. Then we'll repeat the whole set of eight.'

Let me talk about what our first subject did with the poems. After the first poem he produced a description and a rule. The description was that it was a religious poem and the rule was that he wasn't publishing any religious poems. Over the next three presentations he developed three more descriptions, each with its own rule. One was a 'story' poem and he rejected it because 'story poems have to have a moral'. One was a 'descriptive' poem that he accepted because it was 'parsimonious' and descriptive poems should be 'parsimonious of words'. Finally, there was a 'non-descriptive' poem, eventually called 'narrative', that was rejected because it lacked the narrative poem criterion: 'insight into the human condition'. Our naive subject produced an epistemic rule for each ontological category – rules that lack the one-many mapping that distinguishes abstract epistemic structures. But by the last trial he achieved an enormous economy. He dropped the 'story poem' category and its 'moral' rule as well, and kept only the two remaining rules – *parsimony* and *insight*. These now served him as standards for selecting *all* poems, and there was no further need for his earlier categorial distinction between narrative and descriptive poems: 'It's just that the second time through the poems made the distinction between descriptive and narrative harder.' Moreover, our subject now discovered a disjunctive relationship between his two rules: 'What we have here is a *trade-off*. ... If a poem does both well it's easily accepted. If it does either one tremendously well it should be accepted.'

One thing is plain. Rules become more abstract as the material to which they apply becomes more familiar. Early rules that lack generality are dropped and new ones of greater generality enter. In time these are combined, as in the 'trade-off' example. *Trade-off* probably marks the beginning of taking the formerly epistemic rules (insight and parsimony) as ontic objects that can be thought on their own via other rules (trade-off). For 'trade-off' is a rule for dealing with rules. Now 'insight' and 'parsimony' are things to be combined. As these new thought objects become reified, the preceding ontic taxonomy (descriptive and narrative) is dropped. What before were rules for operating, finally become objects of thought.

As adults we have well-learned patterns of given and new, ontic and epistemic for the organization of knowledge. We do not even need to learn how to do an ontic dump in order to move to higher ground in our understanding of unfamiliar matters. Increasing familiarity provides opportunities for comment generation and elaboration, and in fairly short order we are able to 'go meta' on those comments, to subject them to an ontic dump.

I have argued that every cognitive act contains two components: one ontic, the other epistemic. In order to think about something, the something thought about must first be represented in some form in the mind of the person who is to think about it. Creating a representation is described as a constructive process. Often this constructive process converts an earlier epistemic procedure into an ontic object and permits us to move to higher ground by 'ontic dumping'. The development of this duality can be seen in the three contexts we have explored: in the development of an adult conversation, in the entry of a young child into discourse, and in the formulation of rules and concepts in a domain where the subject is becoming gradually at home. All three contexts represent 'developmental' processes in which the steps leading to eventual ontic dumping are evident.

I believe that this duality of ontic and epistemic is basic to thinking. It has its counterpart in language in the crucial distinction between given and new. The parallel between the two – the ontic-epistemic distinction in thought and the given–new in language – may help explain one of the ways in which language is instrumental in shaping thought.

References

Berger, P., and Luckmann, T., *The Social Construction of Reality*. Garden City, NY: Doubleday, 1966.

Bruner, J., Olver, R., and Greenfield, P. *et al.*, *Studies in Cognitive Growth*. New York: Wiley, 1966.

Bickhard, M., and Richie, D.M., *On the Nature of Representation*. New York: Praeger, 1983.

Carey, S., 'Constraints on word meanings – natural kinds'. Unpublished ms, Massachusetts Institute of Technology, 1983.

Feldman, C., and Toulmin, S., 'Logic and the theory of mind', *Nebraska Symposium on Motivation, 1975*. Lincoln: University of Nebraska Press, 1976.

Feldman, C., 'Two functions of language', *Harvard Educational Review*, 1977, 47.

Goodman, N., *Of Mind and Other Matters*. Cambridge, Mass.: Harvard University Press, 1984.

Jakobson, R., *Selected Writings*. The Hague: Mouton, 1981.

Piaget, J., *The Essential Piaget*. New York: Basic Books, 1977.

Steiner, P. (ed.), *The Prague School: Selected Writings 1929–1946*. Austin: University of Texas Press, 1982.

8
Social representations of gender

BARBARA LLOYD

Introduction

Age and sex are fundamental categories in the organization of social life in all human societies. Each of us on first meeting a stranger mentally classifies that individual as a man or woman. Because ageing and sexual differentation are biological processes the social psychological construction of concepts such as young and old, masculine and feminine is easily overlooked.

In this chapter I use the term gender rather than sex to emphasize the constructedness of the category (cf. Archer and Lloyd, 1985). For many years cross-cultural evidence has been advanced to show that gender concepts vary from one society to another (Mead, 1935). Differences in socialization experience have been invoked to account for gender differences in human behaviour but the child's active contribution to the construction of gender categories only began to receive attention with the work of Kohlberg (1966). My own interest in children's construction of gender arose from a study which attempted to assess the influence of socially constructed gender concepts and biological sex on mothers behaviour while playing with an infant (Smith and Lloyd, 1978).

Caroline Smith and I observed mothers of firstborn 6-month-olds as they played with babies who were systematically presented either as a boy or a girl. Ideas of masculinity and femininity guided the behaviour of the mothers we observed. Babies dressed as boys were offered a toy hammer and verbally encouraged to engage in vigorous action. When the same baby was presented as a girl she was shown a fluffy doll and praised for being clever and attractive. Particularly intriguing was a tendency of these mothers to respond with further gross motor behaviour when the baby displaying gross motor behaviour was presented as a boy. We examined the total amounts of gross motor activity among our four 'actor' babies; however, we were unable to detect any statistically reliable evidence of sex-related differences in the motor behaviour of these 6-month-old infants.

Caroline Smith also studied the behaviour of mothers playing with their own firstborns at 6 and 13 months of age (Smith, 1982). During play with their mothers boys at 13 months engaged in more gross motor activity – pushing, pulling and banging objects – while girls made more fine motor responses – fitting objects together or carefully placing them in particular locations. In earlier research Goldberg and Lewis (1969) had found that girls played more with blocks, pegboards and toys with faces. These gender differences at 13 months may reflect babies' experiences at 6 months which are shaped by mothers' social representations of gender. I interpret the 13-month-olds' gender-differentiated toy choice and play styles as evidence that these children are beginning to construct a concept of gender, albeit in practical activity and with some help from their mothers.

I have introduced the term social representations to describe the gender concepts of mothers because it encompasses both symbolic functions and the role of social processes in the construction of reality. Moscovici (1983) defines *social representations* as

> systems of values, ideas and practices with a two-fold function: first, to establish an order which will enable individuals to orient themselves in and master their social world, and second to facilitate communication among members of a community by providing them with a code for naming and classifying the various aspects of their world and their individual and group history.

Even in the interaction of mothers with 6-month-olds there is evidence of the regulation of the material world (toys) according to gender rules. The linguistic communications addressed to these infants appear designed to encourage their entry into their social world equipped with the appropriate gender codes.

I have identified the social representations of mothers as a first step in describing the development of children's understanding of gender. Social representations may be viewed as structured systems which regulate the child's construction of reality just as in Piaget's analysis of cognitive development it is the 'closed structures' of logical systems which regulate the child's (re)construction of logico-mathematical structures. This view of social representations raises important developmental issues which have only recently been addressed (cf. Duveen, 1984; Moscovici and Hewstone, 1983).

The behaviour of 3½-year-old children provides a variety of evidence for regulation in terms of the social representations of gender. Linguistically, their use of gender-marked nouns, such as man/woman, boy/girl, and the pronouns he/she/him/her, is accurate. The categories boy and girl are available for them to label themselves appropriately and to sort pictures of people by gender (Thompson, 1975). Their practical activity is gender marked when appropriate toy choices are made in play (Blakemore, LaRue and Oljnik, 1979; Lloyd and Smith, 1985a).

Neither the development of social representations nor changes in linguistic, cognitive and interpersonal behaviour more generally, have been thoroughly explored in the period between 19 and 42 months old. The research I describe was designed to allow us to sketch the construction of social representations within the domain of gender by children in this age range. I have sought to identify emerging representations of gender in language, in cognitive tasks and in the interpersonal behaviour of children with their mothers and with a familiar peer. Most studies of the development of representational capacities focus on reflective understanding and employ linguistic and cognitive data. The use of play as evidence derives from a belief that children learn about gender through practical activity and that changes in interpersonal behaviour are related to developments in their construction of social representations (Cahill, 1983). My research on the development of social representations of gender is concerned with a specific system of values, ideas and practices, but the emergence of adult-like gender representations depends on and may indeed influence more general linguistic, cognitive and social development in children between 19 and 42 months old.

Elements in the construction of social representations of gender

The elements from which age-specific sketches of children's social representations of gender will be constructed were collected in a multi-faceted study of gender knowledge. The 120 children who participated in the main study ranged in age from 19 to 42 months and were blocked in four age groups.

Although the construction of social representations depends jointly upon linguistic, cognitive and social development the three dimensions can be investigated separately. Tasks designed to test children's ability to recognize and to produce common and gender-marked nouns, e.g. BASKET and DADDY, and gender-marked pronouns, e.g. SHE and HE, assess linguistic development and specifically that relating to the code which social representations of gender provides. Sorting tasks employing differently shaped pieces of red and blue card, and coloured photographs of cats and dogs, of men and women and boys and girls, and of the toys the children were later to play with, measure cognitive development and explore the classificatory function of gender representations.

Interpersonal behaviour, both with mothers and with a familiar peer, was observed in a laboratory room equipped with gender stereotyped toys. The toys were selected on the basis of parental ratings of the gender appropriateness of objects described as boys' and girls' toys in published reports. The array of toys thus reflects the social representations of relevant adults. Videotape records of the play sessions were analysed for action play, pretend play and social behaviour. These behavioural data, which indicate the child's orientation in and mastery of the social world, offer another perspective on the construction of social representations of gender.

In order to compose age-specific sketches of children's social representations of gender I first present descriptive summaries of the elements from which they will be created. These elements are measures of gender-related aspects of linguistic, cognitive and interpersonal behaviour.

Linguistic tasks: labelling

In order to keep the attention of such young children while assessing both their recognition and their capacity to produce words a combined-test strategy was developed. Before each individual test session began, two polaroid pictures of the child were made and inserted into a photographic album containing thirty-six other polaroid pictures. Recognition was tested first by presenting a page of the album containing two photographs and asking the child a question in the form 'Show me the MAN' or 'Which one is HE?' Even if the child failed to choose the photograph of a man, the next question focused on the alternative picture, that of a woman, and the child was asked 'Who is it?' and expected to produce the reply LADY or SHE.

The gender-marked nouns used in these tasks were MUM-MY, DADDY, LADY, MAN, GIRL and BOY. The pronouns were SHE, HE, HER and HIM. Performance on these tasks showed two effects familiar from studies of language development. Older children performed better on all the tasks and production tasks were more difficult at every age. The scores of children in the youngest group and in the second group were significantly different from those of children in all other groups. Gender-marked noun recognition was near perfect, 94 per cent and 99 per cent in the two oldest groups. Even the youngest children were correct 60 per cent of the time. Pronoun recognition was more difficult with 15 per cent correct in the youngest group and only 91 per cent correct in the oldest group. Performance in self-recognition, i.e. applying the correct label GIRL or BOY to own photograph, was similar to that for pronoun recognition.

The difficulty which children in the two younger groups had in applying the gender-marked nouns BOY and GIRL to self photographs may be related to a lack of familiarity with these terms, but this is clearly not the whole explanation. Recognition scores for children in these two groups reached 49 per cent and 73 per cent respectively for the terms BOY and GIRL, but scores for the adult terms, MAN and LADY, were significantly higher.

The superiority of girls was the most consistent finding in the pronoun-recognition results. Both in pilot testing of sixty-four children and in the main study of 120 children this difference was statistically significant.

Scores on production tasks were consistently lower than scores on the corresponding recognition tasks. It was more difficult to score correct responses on production tasks. Having passed the recognition test by pointing to the picture of a woman when asked to 'Show me MUMMY', the child could produce the term DADDY, to the photograph of the man, but many other terms are possible, among them MAN. To account for these possibilities four criteria were used in scoring correct responses. These were (1) gender, (2) age, (3) part of speech, and (4) precision in supplying the particular complement to the recognition item. The marked superiority on the recognition tasks may result from the application of these stringent criteria (cf. Bloom, 1974).

Children in the two youngest groups had great difficulty producing complements for the gender-marked nouns they were generally able to recognize. Percentages of correct replies were 18 and 41 respectively. Children in the oldest group were completely correct only 68 per cent of the time. The youngest children often failed to produce a response but errors which did occur were analysed according to the four-dimensional scoring system. The majority of errors resulted from a failure to meet the specific demands of the test situation, i.e. MAN was produced rather than DADDY. Gender confusion accounted for only 2.4 per cent of errors in the production of gender-marked nouns and age confusion 3.5 per cent. Other dimensions of the linguistic code posed greater difficulty than the understanding of gender marking.

Children identify gender and age in photographs but our test procedure was unsuccessful in prompting the production of gender-marked pronouns in children of this age. There were no completely correct replies in the youngest group and only four from children in the oldest group. After SHE as a recognition item, 75 of the 120 children produced MAN or DADDY rather than HE.

Cognitive tasks: classifying

Children were tested on four sorting tasks. Initially they were asked to put photographs of the fourteen toys they would later encounter in the playroom into two boxes painted to look like houses with the picture of a girl fixed on the door of one and the picture of a boy on the other. Subsequently they sorted six red and blue geometric shapes, and photographs of six cats and dogs, six boys and girls, and six men and women. Each of the four sorting tasks was scored in one of four categories – totally successful, nearly successful, minimal attempt or failure. Performance improved with age and children found it easier to sort for colour and species (cats and dogs) than to sort people or toys according to gender. Girls performed significantly better on all of these tasks. Of the thirty children in the youngest group only one was totally successful in sorting colour, one in sorting species, but no one managed to sort people by gender. In the oldest group 63 per cent of children sorted people correctly by gender; 83 per cent were successful with colour and 90 per cent with species.

Children's ability to sort toys according to gender improved with age and overall girls were again more successful than boys. Boys were better when sorting boys' toys but girls sorted with equal facility despite the stereotypic value of the toys. However, even girls in the oldest group scored barely 60 per cent correct.

Interpersonal behaviour

Interpersonal interaction in play sessions was analysed as action play, pretend play and social behaviour. A computer-assisted recording system (Smith, Lloyd and Crook, 1982) was used to analyse action play and social behaviour. Pretend play was coded from the transcriptions.

Action play Categories in the analysis of action play derived from those used to study 13-month-olds and included (1) hold toy without playing with it, (2) active involvement with toy marked by visual attention as well as physical contact and (3) gross motor activity involving a toy, e.g. banging, pushing or running with a toy. Both the type of play and the toy involved were recorded. Duration measures for each toy were calculated and summed for boys' and girls' toys.

Toy perference in play with mother was not analysed because mothers were instructed to ensure that their children were familiar with all the toys. The gender-marked toy preference of

13-month-olds is repeated in the peer play of children 19 to 42 months of age. Boys spend more time in action play (categories 2 and 3) with boys' toys and girls spend more time playing with girls' toys. The preference of boys for boys' toys increases with age but girls' choice of boys' toys shows no systematic age effect. There are no interpretable age effects for girls' toys. However, own-gender toy choice is weaker in boy/girl pairs. Girls play less with girls' toys and more with boys' toys than girls in girl/girl pairs while boys play less with boys' toys and more with girls' toys in boy/girl pairs.

Boys engage in significantly more gross motor play when duration is analysed across the two settings – play with mother and with a peer. Also, significantly more gross motor play occurs in peer interaction than during play with mother. However, when peer play alone is analysed to compare duration in same gender and boy/girl pairs, the gender difference in gross motor play fails to reach conventional levels of significance ($p = 0.06$).

Pretend play A unit of pretend play was identified when a child showed clearly that fantasy elements which were not inherent in the toy as object were being invoked, e.g. child saying 'This is my baby', while hugging a doll. The motoric component, hugging, was independently coded as action play. Sustained sequences of imaginary gender role play, such as that involved in 'going shopping' or 'cooking a meal', occurred rarely and only in the oldest group. There were ten episodes identifiable as scripted play in this group (Lloyd and Smith, 1985b).

Units of pretend play are rare in the two younger groups. Frequency increases significantly with age and girls create more pretend units than boys. Pretend units first become frequent for girls during play with boys at 3 years of age and units of pretend play are high both in same and mixed gender pairs in the oldest group. Pretend units become frequent among boys only in the oldest group.

Separate statistical analyses of pretend play with boys' toys and girls' toys for children in the oldest group showed that girls create more units of pretend play with girls' toys than boys do and that girls construct fewer units of pretend play with boys' toys when playing in mixed pairs than when playing with another girl. Even in this age group there was no statistically significant preference among boys for boys' toys.

Social behaviour Jacklin and Maccoby (1978) reported that more social behaviour, both negative and positive, is directed to partners of the same gender. Using a category system based upon their work the effect was replicated across the four age groups (Lloyd and Smith, 1986). Not only was social behaviour more frequent in same gender pairs but it increased across the four age groups.

A different picture emerges from analysis of the sub-categories of social behaviour. Although statistically age is highly significant in the analysis of *assertive behaviour*, which includes aggression, attempt to take toy, taking of toy, vocal command and prohibition, it is uninterpretable developmentally. The frequency of *prosocial behaviour*, did not change with age and *withdrawal behaviour*, which includes withdraw toy, refuse, approach mother and protest, declined over the age range.

Children in boy/girl pairs made more *offer toy* and *suggest share* bids, the units which comprise prosocial behaviour. Only this sub-category is more frequent in boy/girl pairs and may reflect a heightened interest in cross gender partners. Age interacts with pair effects in the assertive and withdrawal sub-categories. Age also interacts with gender. Only in the oldest age group do boys display more assertive behaviour than girls and it is only girls in the oldest group who show more withdrawal than boys. Moreover, examination of interactive sequences revealed that boys' assertive bids were significantly more successful than those of girls (Lloyd and Smith, 1986).

Accounting for social representations of gender

The linguistic, cognitive and interpersonal behaviour of children in the youngest group – those approaching 2 years of age – and that of the oldest group – those approaching 3½ years – presents wide contrasts. The gender-noun recognition of children in the youngest group shows that they are beginning to acquire the gender code but they are unable to apply the terms girl/boy to themselves, nor do they recognize gender-marked pronouns. Production of gender-marked nouns and pronouns is beyond them, as are the sorting tasks.

In the practical activity of the youngest children evidence of gender marking is also mixed. Boys play more with boys' toys and girls with girls' toys but in boy/girl pairs gender differentiation in toy choice is not apparent. So too, in gross motor behaviour, for although boys engage in more gross motor activity overall, in play with peers it is not as clearly differentiated.

In all domains the behaviour of 3½-year-olds offers more consistent evidence of the construction of adult-like social representations of gender. Linguistically and conceptually these children not only recognize and employ gender-marked nouns and pronouns, but they are able to use them to label themselves. They can sort people according to gender but sorting toys remains a problem. Toys are differentiated in practical activity. Not only are gender-appropriate toys chosen in action play but girls of this age are more likely to chose gender-appropriate toys in constructing units of pretend play and to eschew boys' toys in pretend play when boys are present. Even the social behaviour of 3½-year-olds shows changes in line with adult gender rules; only in this age group do girls display more withdrawal and boys more assertive behaviour.

These sketches show, as does much developmental research, that older children master many tasks which are beyond the reach of younger children – that their understanding of gender is more similar to adult representations. The consistent gender differences – girls are better at pronoun recognition and sorting, they choose gender-appropriate toys when constructing units of pretend play and this play is sensitive to the presence of an opposite-gender peer – are a more unusual feature. Such differences are not consistently reported in children of this age range.

If the age differences reported here are very much in line with expectations and the gender differences variable across different samples of children, what can be learned from these data beyond their contribution as a description of the gradual construction of social representations of gender? What is their import for developmental social psychology?

Lefebvre-Pinard (1982) lamented methodological difficulties in establishing empirical relationships between the development and organization of knowledge and its use in regulating everyday behaviour. She suggested that the studies which she had undertaken on children of 3 to 5 years may have failed to demonstrate these relationships because the cognitive rules she assessed may have been local or context-bound. The children she studied may have failed to reach a threshold value of rule generalization which would result in any systematic influence on social behaviour. I believe that these findings speak to this issue. They demonstrate that research in a deliberately restricted domain can address questions about the relationships between rules and behaviour.

The possibility of demonstrating links between reflective knowledge and behaviour may be enhanced by focusing attention on a single domain within which thought and action can be assumed to share meaning (Culler, 1976). By introducing a range of tasks, not only those which require the child to generalize abstract rules in order to influence action, and by employing different social settings, the cognitive demands upon the child can be varied within a content-specific domain.

Relationships between gender knowledge and behaviour can be inferred from the action play of the young children I have described. Across the age range there is a systematic, gender-determined toy preference in action play. That this preference breaks down in boy/girl pairs, where interest in the child of the other gender leads to offers and suggestions to share toys, suggests that this knowledge is tied to the immediate interpersonal setting, or to borrow Margaret Donaldson's term (see Chapter 5), is 'physically embedded'. Gender differentiation at the level of action is not yet sufficiently supported by reflective understanding of social representations of gender to overcome the social influence or attenuating effects of other interpersonal interests.

Social representations of gender are 'psychologically embedded' in mothers' thinking and thus function to regulate gender differentiation in their children's behaviour. The analysis of gross motor activity again shows that in young children this differentiation is susceptible to influence by other interpersonal needs. Play with mothering adults may provide a scaffolding of social representations of gender which fosters gender differentiation. In peer play, although there is more gross motor activity, social influence factors lead to behaviour which appears less gender-typed.

The failure of children in the two youngest groups to apply the terms girl/boy to themselves is further evidence of an inability to move beyond the here and now constraints of the immediate situation, of 'physically embedded' thinking. For these children social representations of gender do not yet function as differentiated signifiers which would allow them to apply the terms girl/boy to themselves as readily as they use their own proper names.

Evidence for the influence on behaviour of more generalized gender rules (of 'mentally-embedded' gender thinking) comes from a multivariate analysis with mother or peer as a primary classification and the linguistic and cognitive tasks already described, as co-variates. There were no significant relationships between scores on the linguistic and cognitive tasks and toy choice in play with a peer whether the measures derived from action or pretend play. In pretend play with mother, however, children's scores both on pronoun recognition and people sorting tasks predicted gender appropriate toy choice. This finding offers indirect evidence for the hypothesis that behaviour of mothers, organized in terms of social representations of gender, supports the limited linguistic and cognitive capacities of very young children and allows them to regulate their pretend play behaviour in a gender-appropriate manner. It suggests that even for these children it may be possible to demonstrate a relationship between linguistic–cognitive development and interpersonal behaviour (practical activity) when content and context are carefully specified and when mothers provide necessary support.

These speculations leave many questions. Why is toy choice in pretend play with mother related to pronoun recognition and not to the other linguistic tasks? How are pronoun recognition and gender sorting related? Why should there be relationships between linguistic and cognitive tasks and pretend play but not with action play?

Some of the answers may be found by looking at an analysis of the pattern of interrelations between the various linguistic and cognitive tasks. Scores for children in the main study on ten tasks – three recognition and three production tasks using (a) gender nouns, (b) pronouns and (c) common nouns, and four sorting tasks employing (a) colour, (b) species, (c) people and (d) toys – were factor analysed using a maximum likelihood procedure. Three factors were derived. Only the production of gender nouns, pronouns and common nouns had high loadings on the first factor. Gender-noun recognition and common-noun recognition had high loadings on the third factor. Both of these are linguistic dimensions and if they can be validly separated they suggest processes akin to labelling and recognition. The second factor comprised pronoun recognition, colour, species and gender sorting. Toy sorting failed to load on this factor. The nature of the processes which this factor reveals are not well described by calling it a sorting factor. Intuitively it would appear that the ability to interpret a pronoun by attending to gender but ignoring age and case involves a process akin to keeping in mind a conceptual distinction and applying it to a set of stimuli. I construe this process as analogous to the 'mental embedding' that allows thought about personal concerns outside of the immediate present, which Margaret Donaldson describes in Chapter 5.

Action play is different from pretend play in which language figured prominently in identifying units. The impact of social influence factors on toy choice and gross motor behaviour implies that mentally embedded social representations of gender have only limited influence in regulating the action of children in this age range. Thus it is not surprising to find no relationship between action play and performance on linguistic and cognitive tasks.

A scenario of development can be drawn from this examination of the processes involved in the construction of social representations of gender. Mothers initially employ their social representations of gender in the regulation of their activity and that of their infants. By 18-months the practical activity of children has begun to show evidence of independent gender regulation. These children choose gender appropriate toys and show gender differentiation in gross motor activity. Adult regulation is still necessary to sustain this differentiation. The youngest children are beginning to acquire the gender code but as yet there is little differentiation of the signified (i.e. the social representation of gender) and its signifiers (i.e. the linguistic, cognitive and social interpersonal behaviour described earlier). Therefore, gender knowledge has only limited effect in regulating the practical activity of these children.

Our own difficulties in differentiating the signified and the signifier can hamper research in this domain. The use of gender-appropriate toy choice as a measure of gender differentiation may lead to an underestimation of young children's gender knowledge and of the influence of that knowledge on interpersonal behaviour. Within the here and now situation a girl offering her boy partner a gun may 'know' that boys play with guns but to an observer her behaviour appears to be less gender differentiated. Our research did not explore this possibility. However, when there is *no* prospect of peer interaction the presence of an observing cross-gender partner leads slightly older children to decrease their cross-gender toy choice (cf. Serbin *et al.*, 1979).

Gender-appropriate toy choice in pretend play with mother, pronoun recognition, and sorting by gender are first steps in the regulation of practical activity in terms of the reflective understanding of social representations of gender. There is evidence that mothering adults provide a scaffolding and the behaviour of girls in the oldest group indicates the nature of the child's subsequent achievement (Wood, Bruner and Ross, 1976). The conceptual precocity of these girls, which is shown in their performances on the pronoun recognition and sorting tasks, also finds expression in their interpersonal behaviour. They not only systematically choose girls' toys when constructing pretend units but they are less likely to use boys' toys in pretend play when boys are present. In other words, their behaviour begins to show the regulation of action by a reflective understanding of the gender rule system.

This examination of the construction of social representations of gender only hints at the complexity of the interplay of developmental forces. Not only is linguistic, cognitive and interpersonal development intertwined but our success in observing change is influenced by our capacity to employ social representations of gender in creating the settings and tasks appropriate to measure its development. Perhaps by narrowing attention to a single, ecologically important concept in social life we can maximize our chances of manipulating, measuring and understanding cognitive social development.

Acknowledgements

The research reported here was made possible by support from the Social Science Research Council, Grant no. HR 5871.

I would like to thank Gerard Duveen, Peter Lloyd and Caroline Smith for their comments on earlier drafts of this chapter. It has also benefited from the scrutiny of the editors.

References

Archer, J., and Lloyd, B., *Sex and Gender* (rev. edn). New York: Cambridge University Press, 1985.

Blakemore, J.E.O., LaRue, A.A., and Oljnik, A.B., 'Sex-appropriate toy preference and the ability to conceptualize toys as sex-role related', *Developmental Psychology*, 1979, 15, 339–40.

Bloom, L., 'Talking, understanding and thinking', in R.L. Schiefelbusch and L.L. Lloyd (eds), *Language Perspective: Acquisition, Retardation, and intervention*. New York: Macmillan, 1974.

Cahill, S.E., 'Re-examining the acquisition of sex roles: a social interactionist approach', *Sex Roles*, 1983, 9, 1–15.

Culler, J., *Saussure*. London: Fontana, 1976.

Donaldson, M., 'The origins of inference'. Paper read at the British Association for the Advancement of Science, Salford, September 1980.

Duveen, G.M., 'From social cognition to the cognition of social life: An essay in decentration'. Unpublished D.Phil. thesis, University of Sussex, 1984.

Goldberg, S., and Lewis M., 'Play behavior in the year-old infant, early sex differences', *Child Development*, 40, 21–31, 1969.

Grief, E.B., 'Sex role playing in pre-school children', reprinted in J.S. Bruner, A. Jolly and K. Sylva (eds), *Play: Its Role in Development and Evolution*. Harmondsworth: Penguin, 1976.

Jacklin, C.N., and Maccoby, E.E., 'Social behaviour at 33 months in same-sex and mixed-sex dyads', *Child Development*, 1978, 49, 557–69.

Kohlberg, L., 'A cognitive developmental analysis of children's sex role concepts and attitudes', in E.E. Maccoby (ed.), *The Development of Sex Differences*. Stanford, Calif: Stanford University Press, 1966.

Lefebvre-Pinard, M., 'Questions about the relationship between social

162   *Making Sense*

cognition and social behaviour: the search for the missing link', *Canadian Journal of Behavioural Science*, 1982, 14, 323–37.

Lloyd, B., and Smith, C., 'The social representation of gender and young children's play', *British Journal of Developmental Psychology*, 1985a, 3, 65–73.

Lloyd, B., and Smith, C., 'Gender scripts: children's understanding of gender and gender-marked play'. Paper read at the Developmental Psychology Section Conference, British Psychological Society, Belfast, September, 1985b.

Lloyd, B., and Smith, C., 'The effects of age and gender on social behaviour in very young children', *British Journal of Social Psychology*, 1986, 25, 33–41.

Mead, M., *Sex and Temperament*. New York: William Morrow, 1935.

Moscovici, S., 'Social representation', in R. Harre and R. Lamb (eds), *The Encyclopedic Dictionary of Psychology*. Oxford: Blackwell, 1983.

Moscovici, S., and Hewstone, M., 'Social representation and social explanation: from the "naive" to the "amateur" scientist', in M. Hewston (ed.), *Attribution Theory*. Oxford: Blackwell, 1983.

Schau, C.G., Kahn, L., Diepold, J.H., and Cherry, F., 'The relationships of parental expectations and preschool children's verbal sex typing to their sex-typed toy play behavior', *Child Development*, 1980, 51, 266–70;.

Serbin, L., Connor, J.M., Burchardt, C.J., and Citron, C.C., 'Effects of peer presence on sex-typing of children's play behavior', *Journal of Experimental Child Psychology*, 1979, 27, 303–9.

Smith, C., 'Mothers' attitudes and behaviour to infants and the development of sex-typed play'. Unpublished doctoral dissertation, University of Sussex, 1982.

Smith, C., and Lloyd, B.B., 'Maternal behavior and perceived sex of infant', *Child Development*, 1978, 49, 1263–5.

Smith, C., Lloyd, B.B., and Crook, C., 'Instrumentation and software report: computer assisted coding of videotape material', *Current Psychological Research*, 1982, 2, 289–92.

Terman, L.M., and Merrill, M.A., *Stanford-Binet Intelligence Scale: Manual for the Third Revision. Form L–M*. Boston: Houghton-Mifflin, 1960.

Thompson, S.K., 'Gender labels and early sex-role development', *Child Development*, 1975, 46, 339–47.

Wood, D., Bruner, J.S., and Ross, G., 'The role of tutoring in problem-solving', *Journal of Child Psychology and Psychiatry*, 1976, 17, 89–100.

9

Growing into rules

HELEN HASTE

'You shouldn't hit people; it hurts.'

'When our family played Monopoly, you could collect rent when you were in jail.'

'Real men don't eat quiche.'

Such rules are the grammar of social relations. They are a model for ordering and organizing one's experience; they reflect, and prescribe, a range of explanations of the social and physical world. In acquiring these rules, the child learns the basis for interaction with others, and the shared cultural framework for making sense of the world.

In this chapter I shall explore the ways in which the child grows into an understanding of these grammars, and the ways they are presented to the child in her interaction with the world. I shall draw examples from anthropology and from social and developmental psychology. Specifically, I shall look at three areas of psychological research in which both social and developmental psychologists have worked, and I will consider how, by putting these different approaches together, we can understand individual development within a social and cultural context. These fields of work are, firstly, the development of understanding of moral and conventional rules, secondly, the development of map-making and the rules for representation of

three-dimensional space and, thirdly, the grammar for conceptual differentiation of health and illness.

Obviously there are different kinds of 'rules' in each of these
three fields. Moral and conventional rules are *prescriptive*.
Map-making involves rules for the representation of symbols;
these rules are about *description*. The criteria for differentiating
health and illness are both *descriptive* (or normative) and
evaluative. Bruner has distinguished between 'paradigmatic'
and 'narrative' processes; the former is finding out about the
rule, the latter is accounting for the rule (Bruner, 1986). The
child must first learn what the rule is, but she must also learn
what counts as a legitimate *explanation* or *justification* for the
rule. Only when she is equipped with both of these grammars
for understanding can she decode the social rules she encounters, and participate in communication with others who share
the common grammar.

The examples at the beginning illustrate this. The statement,
'You shouldn't hit people; it hurts' is a prescription, implying a
restraint or control of behaviour. It is also generalizable –
'people' means *any* people. The narrative component, the
qualifying statement that 'it hurts', implies that hurting is bad,
and that hurting is an *adequate justification* for not hitting. And
indeed, the very fact that the individual bothered to give a
justification for the rule shows that presenting explanations for
prescriptive rules is part of the grammar. One of the major
characteristics of prescriptive rules is that they carry sanctions,
and they must be justified by reference to certain classes of
consequence. So, one should not hit because it hurts – or maybe
because one will be punished, or bring disgrace to one's family.
The class of consequence that 'counts' as a justification will
depend on local cultural conditions, as well as upon more
general and universal principles, such as not harming others.

There is a further hidden grammar of prescriptive rules;
prescription implies a gap between 'ought' and 'is'; the
existence of 'ought' statements implies that there is an ideal
state to be aspired to. Most prescriptive rules therefore imply a
tension between what is normative and what is desirable.

The second statement, about the game of Monopoly, is
normative, specifically applied to a narrow category of persons,
the speaker's family. The very expression implies some recogni-

tion of possible relativity – the person has not said, for example 'The rules say . . .'. It is in the nature of commercial games like Monopoly that the official rules get lost and that families and peer groups establish local variations; thus even formal, invented games take on the rule flexibility of traditional games like marbles, hopscotch, tag. As Piaget has shown, part of the child's developing understanding of the rules is appreciating the social mechanisms for agreeing on a normative rule that makes the game playable and 'fair' (Piaget, 1932). The example of collecting rent (or not) while in jail is particularly significant because the chance element in Monopoly is altered by it; peers who differ about this norm must negotiate a consensus at the start for the game to be played at all!

Normative rules also provide a description of the world: 'we get up at half-past seven', 'we keep the paints by the sink', 'girls wear dresses but boys don't'. Such rules are a grammar for *making order*; the child receives the message from such rules that one *can* order one's world and make it predictable. The consequences of breaking such rules is that order is disturbed. That consequence alone may act as sufficient explanation, but in practice most normative rules also imply a functionalist account – it is *necessary* to do things this way or they won't work. A game cannot be played if the rules are not followed; you can't find the paints if they aren't put away properly; if men and women do not have different roles, family life would not be feasible. So the child learns the hidden message that normative rules are legitimated by *functional* explanations.

The third quote is the title of a humorous book about male roles. It states both a normative and prescriptive rule, and it has, further, a strong evaluative connotation. The implications of this statement are (1) that quiche-eating is normatively associated with women, and (2) that men can be divided into 'real' men and 'other' men. The evaluative tone of the statement implies a prescriptive element, but the prescription concerns acceptability and conforming, and affirming the current social categories, rather than the individual's conformity of a moral principle or rule. So, 'proper' boys don't cry, 'nice' girls aren't rough, 'polite' people don't swear; all these are descriptions, but they carry the connotation that it is important to be proper, nice and polite, and that such epithets (or their negatives) are the legitimate basis for defining people in positive or negative terms. This process of categorization has been particularly explored in the work of Tajfel and his associates in the study of intergroup relations. They demonstrated that the process of categorization into 'ingroup' and 'outgroup' – which may be on the most trivial of criteria – is closely interwoven with the use of evaluative labels and symbols (Tajfel, 1981). So in acquiring the rules of evaluation, the child is learning, firstly, the basis for social categorization of people (and things) in positive or negative terms and, secondly, the epithets which are used within her culture to express such evaluations appropriately. Such epithets frequently – as in the example above – involve evoking the behaviour or characteristics of an antithetical or negatively evaluated group; so the child learns to ridicule boys by ascribing to them the attributes of girls, older children by ascribing to them the attributes of younger children. According to local conditions, religious and ethnic groups are categorized in similar style.

The social and the individual

The developmental processes by which the child becomes competent in decoding the grammar of rules include both social and individual dimensions. The social dimensions are the ways in which rules are manifested in social interactions and in social structures. At the level of individual behaviour, these are represented in actions and rituals for interactions. Thus the child learns how to *enact* the rule before she can express it or make it conscious and articulated. But the social dimension also includes the fact that rules develop generally within the social and cultural world, and that rules and their meaning are negotiated and perpetuated amongst groups and institutions of society.

The individual dimension is the development of the child's competence in making cognitive sense of the world, and in engaging effectively in interaction with others. This involves the structural bases of the individual child's thinking, and the processes which affect the development and the transfomation of the child's own construction of meaning.

The social and individual dimensions of growing into rules

have been studied and analysed within the disparate and largely non-overlapping theoretical models of social and developmental psychology. There has latterly been the beginnings of rapprochement, however, influenced by the revival of interest in Vygotsky's work; this I will explore in detail. But let us first consider the nature of the conflict between social and developmental approaches.

Bourdieu writes as an anthropologist; his research illustrates particularly vividly the structural and action framework of social rules (Bourdieu, 1977). He studied the Kabylia, a North African peasant society. The Kabylia practise social interaction in a heavily symbolicized way: greeting behaviours, for example – and the act of failing to greet – reflect very precisely the social status of the individual. The management of giving and receiving gifts is carefully orchestrated to express honour. In Kabylia society, the roles of males and females are sharply circumscribed, and maintaining their relative status is a complex and crucial part of every aspect of social life and ritual. The metaphor and symbolism associated with gender marking are very extensive, and gender dualism is represented by many metaphoric polarities such as public/private, open/secret, proud/shameful, light/dark. These are expressed in language, in forms of social interaction and in power relations; also the utilization of space, both within the house and in the public domain, expresses gender categorization very explicitly.

Such action-structured relations, and their attendant symbolism, are part of most societies but they are particularly marked amongst the Kabylia. In every domain of action a complex symbolism is involved in interpreting this practice. This grammar of action, practice and interpretation must be acquired by the growing child. Bourdieu says:

Practice always implies a cognitive operation, a practical operation of construction which sets to work, by reference to practical functions, systems of classification (taxonomies) which organise preception and structure practice. Produced by the practice of successive generations, in conditions of existence of a determinate type, these schemes of perception, appreciation and action, which are acquired through practice and applied in their practical state without acceding to explicit representation, function as practical operators through which the objective structures of which they are a product tend to reproduce themselves in practice. (1977, p. 97)

Thus, children learn through their own action and interaction the significance of the different parts of the space they occupy, and they come to understand, enact and reenact the grammar of these social rules through indirect linguistic means – such as proverbs – and through direct and explicit representation.

As with the Kabylia, of course, so with all societies. The particular value to the present discussion of Bourdieu's analysis is that it integrates an anthropological perspective on the society as a whole, and an account of individual and interpersonal psychology which recognizes the role of individual cognition in the interpretative process. Meaning and implicit theories about social relations are revealed in the *practice* of members of the society; the *resources* for the child's understanding of the grammar of rule are represented symbolically by the culture, and within this framework of metaphor, symbol and action the child develops her own understanding.

Moscovici and the social psychologists of the 'French School' look at the grammar of rules for categorizing, explaining and legitimating as they are manifested in social processes, but they are mainly interested in the ways that such 'social representations' are expressed in language (Farr and Moscovici, 1984). These are the shared – or negotiated – frameworks of meaning, metaphor and common explanation by which individuals make sense of their experience and are able to communicate with others. Such social representations endure over time within a culture, and are transmitted across generations, like the practices that Bourdieu describes. They also reflect social change; much of the work of the French School is the analysis of the social psychological processes by which meaning is generated *and modified*, and the functions that social representation plays in the definition of group boundaries. Moscovici's classic study of this phenomenon is the demonstration of how the language and concepts of psychoanalysis have become part of the commonsense explanations of French laypeople (Moscovici, 1961/76). We will later look in detail at Herzlich's work on the social representation of health and illness (Herzlich, 1973). Recent work by Jodelet *et al.* shows how social representations are modified in the course of social change; changes in the conception of women's role have been accompanied by changing representations of the body (Jodelet *et al.*, 1980).

Both Bourdieu and the French School of social psychologists focus on the *social origins* of meaning, and the frameworks which the culture provides for making sense and giving legitimation to rules. Their work illustrates that there is a *body of cultural and social resources* which frame the individual's understanding of rules, of the parameters of legitimation and appropriate evaluation, and of the local 'rules-for-making-rules'. Developmental psychologists have concentrated the processes by which the child constructs meaning as an *individual*, and how this process of construction becomes more complex and qualitatively different in the course of development. The rule may exist as a *social fact*, but what interests the developmental psychologist is the developing cognitive capacity of the child to *decode* that social fact, and to appreciate the basis for rule-making.

There now exists a large body of data on the development of the child's construction of a variety of rules, which illustrates qualitative changes of development. Certain common patterns emerge. The child first accepts the rule as given, and justifications for the rule are arbitrary appeals to authority. She then comes to appreciate that rules have the social function of making interaction possible; initially this is an understanding of intra-individual interactions, later it becomes an appreciation of group and community. Finally she can see beyond the conventional rule system and can perceive the wider social structure, so she understands the principles upon which the rule is based, and can herself derive principles for the generation of rules. The data from which these developmental patterns of cognition emerge include rules for games, moral rules, conventional rules, rules for the government of friendship, rules for the categorization of sex roles and rules for the exchange of money. In other words, they include descriptive, prescriptive and evaluative rules, and cover a wide range of social interaction and the interpretation of social experience (Piaget, 1932; Furth, 1978; Damon, 1977; Leahy, 1983; Kohlberg, 1984).

For the developmental psychologist, therefore, 'growing into rules' means increasing cognitive comprehension of the grammar of justification and explanation. The focus of research is upon the individual's construction of meaning, and the changes which take place in cognitive structure. The social context is an *implicit* resource, but the emphasis is on the *individual* operating cognitively upon that resource; *transforming* the rule, its justification and explanation, according to her current cognitive capacity. However, cognitive developmentalists have recently directed more attention to the role of social processes in the child's construction of meaning, especially the role of the interaction between peers. In part, this shift arose from a dissatisfaction with the Piagetian model of the lone child discovering concepts for herself while playing with pebbles on the beach. Damon, for example, argues:

> Categories of the world – whether social *or* physical – are not derived by the child in social isolation, but are worked out in the course of innumerable social exchanges. In the course of these social exchanges, the child's attention is drawn to particular aspects of subject–object relations that have special social and cultural meaning. In this manner, the child's cognitive development is continually guided by the social context in which all knowledge is presented and created. Thus it is more accurate to say that knowledge is 'co-constructed' by the child in relation to others than that it is simply constructed unilaterally. This is equally true of social and physical knowledge. (1981, pp. 162–3)

Damon (1977) has himself studied the ways that children interact in small groups; he observed how they negotiated amongst themselves the allocation of rewards for a completed task. Participation in such small-group conflict can stimulate cognitive disequilibrium, such that there is measurable change over time in the structure of thinking. But more interesting for the present discussion, Damon's study demonstrates the complex social and cognitive processes by which children engage in the negotiation of meaning, of justification and legitimation, and of the basis for establishing criteria for the allocation of rewards. The italicized statements reflect different kinds of justification being invoked for the 'fair' distribution of candy bars; the fact of their being invoked shows that they are part of those children's 'resources' for generating rules for fairness.

The setting is three 10-year-olds who are deciding how to allocate candy bars among a group of themselves plus one other, Dennis; they have been making bracelets:

E (Experimenter): We talked with you all and couldn't decide, so we thought you should decide together. What do you think is the *best way to give it out*?

Craig: Would Dennis get some?

E: If you think so.

Norman: He has to be here too.

E: Well, you all decide among you.

Bonnie: I was thinking, we could give it out one a bracelet, because Dennis did one and we all did three. Or give two and a half to everybody. *That way everybody gets the same thing*.

Craig: Maybe Dennis should get one and we get three.

Norman: *No, it isn't fair*.

Bonnie: Also, *Dennis is younger* and he left earlier.

E: Well, what do you think? Is that the best way?

Norman: No.

E: Why not, Norman?

Norman: Because if he were here too, *and he's a child too, so he should get even* (material omitted).

E: So far you've got one for Dennis, three for you Craig, three for Norman and three for you Bonnie.

Bonnie: (mumbles something) That's what Dennis should get.

Norman: No. He's not, that's what I'm getting at. *That's what I'm putting in your mind, in your mind, in his mind* (pointing to each member in group).

Bonnie: Well, let's split these in half. Everybody gets two and a half.

Norman: Right ... *It's the best way, everyone gets the same amount*.

Bonnie: Craig's is the prettiest, Norman's is the neatest, and I did the most.

Norman: *I was the most well behaved* (material omitted).

Norman: *You're not putting Dennis' mind into your little mind ... I know how he would feel ... Well, you're not reasoning about*

> *him. If we did that he would say* (whiny voice) *'Come, you guys
> got this and I only got that' and he'd start bawling.* (Damon,
> 1977, pp. 128–30, italics added)

Doise and Mugny have demonstrated that children working in
pairs and groups in the solution of logical problems produce
more adequate solutions than when they are working alone
(Doise and Mugny, 1984). Such work emphasizes the continual
interaction between internal cognitive processes and external
social processes. But the question remains, what exactly is the
nature of this interaction? Doise and Mugny, for example, argue
that Piaget's concept of 'reflecting abstraction'

> is an adequate description of the psychological level of what
> occurs in the individual, but integration of earlier regulators
> within new structures must also be studied at the social level
> – the collective elaboration of new structures reorganises
> pre-existing individual abilities. To profit from these collec-
> tive integrations resulting in more advanced structures,
> individuals must already possess the necessary constituent
> elements. (1984, p. 27)

According to this description, the social process operates as
both a *catalyst* and a *consolidator* for individual thinking; the
child cannot do all the work by herself, the process of
negotiation with peers provides a scaffold for the reconstructive
process, and it is the confrontation with externally derived
conflict which stimulates internal disequilibrium.

So, this position is essentially a modification of Piaget's
model, to take account of the social world as a *variable operating
upon individual cognition*. In contrast, Vygotsky argued that the
social process is *prior* to the individual process, not merely a
mediator of it:

> Any function in the child's cultural development appears
> twice, or on two planes. First it appears on the social plane,
> and then on the psychological plane. First it appears between
> people as an interpsychological category, and then within the
> child as an intrapsychological category. This is equally true
> with regard to voluntary attention, logical memory, the
> formation of concepts, and the development of volition.
> (1978, p. 163)

Vygotsky thus places far greater emphasis on the role of interpersonal social process and also upon the role of society, in defining a framework of meaning. For Vygotsky, the 'social' world operates at two levels; firstly at the interpersonal level at which the child, through the medium of language as well as through action, experiences concepts-in-practice. This is the idea of the 'zone of proximal development' – the gap between the social and the intrapsychological experience of a concept – which has gained such currency recently amongst developmental psychologists. But there is another level of analysis, relatively undeveloped because of Vygotsky's untimely death, which I shall argue is of great importance to a rapprochement between developmental and social psychology (Wertsch, 1985).

From Vygotsky's Marxist background came the concept of the *sociohistorical system* within which cultural meaning develops over time. The sociohistorical system provides a framework for thinking and planning, and delineates the tools which are available for these. So according to this, the child's experience in interpersonal interaction, and her own intrapersonal reflection and consolidation of concepts, must ultimately be seen within the wider context of a sociohistorical framework which defines what is possible, what is legitimate and what is, also, functional to the social system. So I interpret Vygotsky as arguing that the process of 'generating meaning' operates at *three* levels; the sociohistorical, the interpersonal and the intra-individual.

So far, I have illustrated a variety of perspectives on the process of 'growing into rules'. We have seen how from an anthropologist's point of view, rules and their justification and legitimations are structurally embedded within action and interaction, language and metaphor, and the child accesses the cultural framework through action as well as through language. This perspective does not offer much role for the child's own construction of meaning, but Bourdieu does acknowledge that the child is active in making cognitive sense of what is going on. The social psychological model of Moscovici demonstrates how, in response to the needs of particular groups and to the demands of social change, there emerges a framework for making sense through collective negotiation of meaning. This framework provides metaphors, explanations and legitimations for both social rules and rules for categorization. The cognitive developmentalists have shown unequivocally that the child's comprehension of the rule and its justifications change in the course of development; thus, whatever the consensual meaning framework within a culture, the child will only imperfectly comprehend it until she reaches the necessary level of cognitive complexity. The cognitive-developmental approach also acknowledges that social interaction at the dyadic and small-group level is important for the child's experience of concepts in use, but this does not, on the whole, incorporate the implications of the *broader* interaction of the child in the social system. Indeed, both Kohlberg and Piaget have been criticized for taking an essentially absolutist position: that their final stages of reasoning, in moral and logical thinking, reflect a universal framework for conceptualization within those domains. Such a view, would have no room for the analysis of the dialectical processes which become evident when one takes a broader perspective of social and historical factors in individual development (Riegel and Rosenwald, 1975; Modgil and Modgil, 1986).[1]

In Figure 9.1 I present a model for conceptualizing the range of perspectives discussed above, and consider possible interactions between the three domains.[2]

In brief, the *intra-individual* is the domain colonized by cognitive developmentalists; the activity of the individual in reflecting, consolidating, constructing. The *interpersonal* domain is the area of dyadic and small-group interaction, where

1   A particularly significant critique of the self-reflective model of cognitive development is by Youniss (1981). Youniss proposes that the development of children's cognitive understanding depends on the relationship in which discourse takes place: the child not only *encounters* concepts in the interpersonal context which stimulate individual thought, but also *generates* concepts in the group context. This is a model of social construction and social negotiation which has many similarities with the work of the French School. However, a further dimension which Youniss introduces is Habermas' theory of the development of communicative competence (Habermas, 1979). The child not only develops cognitive competence (an intrapsychological process) but also passes through stages of interpsychological development. So the process of intraspsychological development is in dialectical relationship with the development of the child's competence reciprocally to interact with others in discourse, in the generation of mutually comprehensible meaning.

2   This model was originally discussed in a paper published some years ago, but at that time I did not appreciate the significance of Vygotsky's work (Weinreich Haste, 1984).

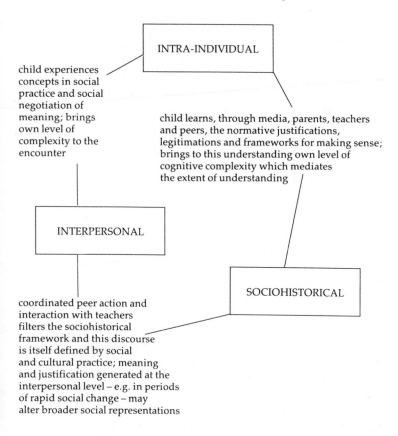

child experiences concepts in social practice and social negotiation of meaning; brings own level of complexity to the encounter

INTRA-INDIVIDUAL

child learns, through media, parents, teachers and peers, the normative justifications, legitimations and frameworks for making sense; brings to this understanding own level of cognitive complexity which mediates the extent of understanding

INTERPERSONAL

SOCIOHISTORICAL

coordinated peer action and interaction with teachers filters the sociohistorical framework and this discourse is itself defined by social and cultural practice; meaning and justification generated at the interpersonal level – e.g. in periods of rapid social change – may alter broader social representations

Figure 9.1 A model of the relationship between the intra-individual, the interpersonal and the sociohistorical
Source: Weinreich Haste, 1984.

the child participates in the social interactions which are the experience of a concept-in-action, and where the negotiation of meaning with others creates disequilibration in her own cognitive structures. From such interactions also the child receives information about the cultural and social framework; the way that children rigidly enforce gender stereotypes amongst themselves, for example, owes more to caricatures of cultural norms than to the real expectations of the social world, as many a conscientiously non-sexist parent finds.

The *sociohistorical* domain is the world of cultural *mores*, culturally defined and expected justification and explanation. The child comes into contact with it through symbols, metaphor and codes for action which *reflect* meaning and social categories, as well as through direct instruction by parents, peers and the media. It delineates the scope and boundaries for the generation of rules and their justifications. It is a resource for the rules for conducting *interpersonal* interaction, as well as for how one should engage in *intrapersonal* reflection upon rules and order. A two-way process is involved; the child's interpretations of the sociohistorical resource depend on her level of cognitive complexity. In our interaction with children we unconsciously manipulate the interaction between cultural resources and individual levels of complexity; we present to them particular messages, particular frameworks within which to make sense of the world, but we adjust the level of that message to the child's level of comprehension. So the child learns two things; the *content* of the message (which will endure) and the appropriate *structure* for conceptualizing it, which we as parents or teachers have presented as a scaffold for understanding, but which we expect to change with increasing maturity. So, for example, as parents we may have the capacity for stage 4 moral reasoning in Kohlberg's terms, but we will offer the child a justification of (say) promise-keeping appropriately formulated to be comprehensible within her stage 2 understanding; we will *eventually* expect her to develop a higher stage of reasoning about the enduring value, promise-keeping.

But it is not only the *content* of a message which is a resource; there are cultural expressions of the different levels of structural complexity found in individual development. One illustration of this comes from a dissertation by Richard Tuffin (1982). He analysed newspaper editorial material and the letters to the editor concerning the mercy-killing of a severely handicapped child. He demonstrated that the 'quality' papers (*The Times, Guardian*) presented arguments couched in higher stages of reasoning – as measured by the Kohlberg scale – than did the tabloids (*Daily Express, Daily Mirror*). He also showed that a skilled journalist presented the same *content* of an argument in different stage-structural terms when writing for different newspapers. The implication of this work is that levels of complexity of reasoning are not simply the properties of individual thought, but are also part of the resources of the culture. The growing child can find justification and explanations expressed at different levels of cognitive structure, within the media and the social environment.

In the remainder of this chapter, I shall explore ways of integrating the work of social psychologists, who have concentrated on the interpersonal and sociohistorical aspects of the model I presented above, and the work of developmental psychologists on the intra-individual and interpersonal dimensions. I shall explore three different kinds of 'rule': prescriptive rules concerning moral and conventional behaviour, descriptive rules concerning the representation of space in maps, and evaluatively-loaded descriptive rules concerning the distinction between health and illness.

Prescriptive rules

Turiel discovered that even very young children are able to distinguish between 'moral' and 'conventional' rules, and he has established the sequence of stages of development within the domain of conventional reasoning. It is clear that structurally (i.e. in terms of cognitive complexity and of the growing appreciation of the perspective of others and of the function of rules in the social system) the two domains are parallel (Turiel, 1983). Turiel's stages are presented in Table 9.1.

The distinction between conventional and moral rules is understood very early. Children appreciate that *moral* rules transcend local conditions, whereas *conventional* rules are relativistic. The standard type of question used to elicit the distinction is, 'Suppose there was a school in which x behaviour is allowed, would it be all right to do it?' When 'x' involves harming – for example hitting – or other 'moral' issues, the child does not consider it permissible even if authority figures or peer norms apparently condone it. However, conventions such as the wearing or not wearing of clothes, or eating with one's fingers, are seen as alterable.

I consider that Turiel's work is particularly interesting because it illustrates the operation of a sociohistorical dimen-

Table 9.1 Major changes in social–conventional concepts

	Approximate ages
1 *Convention as descriptive of social uniformity.* Convention viewed as descriptive of uniformities in behaviour. Convention is not conceived as part of structure or function of social interaction. Conventional uniformities are descriptive of what is assumed to exist. Convention maintained to avoid violation of empirical uniformities.	6–7
2 *Negation of convention as descriptive social uniformity.* Empirical uniformity not a sufficient basis for maintaining conventions. Conventional acts regarded as arbitrary. Convention is not conceived as part of structure or function of social interaction.	8–9
3 *Convention as affirmation of rule system; early concrete conception of social system.* Convention seen as arbitrary and changeable. Adherence to convention based on concrete rules and authoritative expectations. Conception of conventional acts not coordinated with conception of rule.	10–11
4 *Negation of convention as part of rule system.* Convention now seen as arbitrary and changeable regardless of rule. Evaluation of rule pertaining to conventional act is coordinated with evaluation of the act. Conventions are 'nothing but' social expectations.	12–13
5 *Convention as mediated by social system.* The emergence of systematic concepts of social structure. Convention as normative regulation in system with uniformity, fixed roles and static hierarchical organization.	14–16

Table 9.1 Major changes in social–conventional concepts

	Approximate ages
6 *Negation of convention as societal standards.* Convention regarded as codified societal standards. Uniformity in convention is not considered to serve the function of maintaining social system. Conventions are 'nothing but' societal standards that exist through habitual use.	17–18
7 *Conventions as coordination of societal interactions.* Conventions as uniformities that are functional in coordinating social interactions. Shared knowledge, in the form of conventions, among members of social groups facilitates interaction and operation of the system.	18–25

Source: Turiel, 1983.

sion at the level of individual reasoning. As Turiel points out, the distinction between moral and conventional rules is of necessity culturally defined; the child does not generate the distinction herself, even though Turiel finds that children even younger than 3 years can operate with it. In discussing the social origins of rules and their justification, Durkheim distinguished between *moral prescriptions* – such as killing – which had symbolic meaning and were *per se* associated with the obligatory, the valued or the sacred, and did not need to be justified in terms of consequences, they and *prudential laws* which were justified in terms of their consequences. In practice, Turiel's findings indicate that American children do consider the consequences of moral transgression, but these are characterized by an absolute quality and an appeal to a universal principle (such as not hurting). Older children are also able to consider the consequences of both moral and conventional transgressions in terms of their effects on the wider society. So, first the child acquires the *knowledge* that there is a difference; second, the child learns to recognize and to reproduce the distinction in terms of the kinds of *justification* given for rules in the different domains. These justifications are subject to the constraints of the child's level of reasoning.

The different kinds of justification and explanation in conventional reasoning are illustrated in an extract from one of Turiel's interviews with older adolescents on gender roles. The conflict presented in the dilemma concerned the location of jobs; in the past, the woman has subsumed her career interests to her husband's; now she has the opportunity of a very good job which would involve him in moving:

Andrew (14 years): They both have the right, but in the family he probably thinks he does and they go by that.
(what do you mean)
Well he probably thinks he is the main breadwinner and everything . . . when you get married you don't want to have to have your wife work, it is a sign of weakness.
(why is it a sign of weakness)
Because he thinks he can support them himself and he is doing good enough for himself. . . . Because if it comes down to which one should work, he should because he's the man and she should stay at home and you know, say they move and she's working and they have kids, and she's going to work and the guys stays at home with the kids, that's not right.

Elsewhere in the transcript, Andrew has acknowledged that his view of sex roles is not necessarily universally held, but he nevertheless invokes in his argument certain prescriptive statements about 'rightness' and the general obligations of men and women. He cites one set of justifications and explanations that he knows to be acceptable within his culture – the role of breadwinner, the connotation of weakness, the identity of work with the male role and childcare with the female role. He presents a consistent picture. Other respondents produced equally consistent, equally legitimate arguments in support of a more egalitarian view of sex roles. All utilized *cultural resources* in support of a variety of currently acceptable solutions. Their understanding of the dilemma, therefore, and their presentation of a solution, were shaped by and reflect a range of available cultural norms.

Turiel's work bridges developmental and social psychological approaches; he explicitly recognizes and discusses the role of sociohistorical factors in the distinction between conventional and moral reasoning; later I will consider the material he presents concerning interpersonal processes, which gives some insight into the way that the sociohistorical framework becomes transformed and constructed at the intra-individual level.

Another study which illustrates the relationship between intra-individual processes and sociohistorical processes was done in Israel by Nisan (Nisan, 1988). The norms of kibbutz adolescents are egalitarian; the norms of city adolescents favour rewarding effort. Nisan studied adolescents' responses to a dilemma concerning the allocation of rewards in a situation where candidates had shown different degrees of effort. He found the responses of the two groups were *structurally* equivalent, in the sense that they were of the same level of cognitive complexity but they reflected the norms of their group in the *kinds of arguments* (content) invoked. The effect of such normative pressures was that an individual might logically conclude that a particular action or decision was correct, on the basis of her *structural* reasoning, but that powerful cultural norms could override the individual's own reasoning and dictate a response more in tune with the justifications considered legitimate within the sub-culture.

This study is an important demonstration of the separate and possibly conflicting role of intra-individual processes and sociohistorical processes in moral reasoning. It indicates that there must be a *dialectical relationship* between individual and social determinism, and that an explanation in terms of either one or the other is not adequate.

Descriptive rules

Map-making requires the application of descriptive rules governing the representation of space in two dimensions. This is another field at the interface of the intra-individual and the sociohistorical; how does the child come to be able to comprehend and utilize the conventions for symbolizing spatial relations, which involves the capacity to abstract and formalize? Feldman has extended Piaget's work on the intra-individual development of map-making skills and symbolic representation of two-dimensional space (Feldman, 1980).

In the fifteenth century, hardly anyone could draw maps. This was partly due to limited instrumentation, but it was also due to the lack of common code for the representation of distance and spatial relations. Today, almost every child in Western society is exposed to the conventional representation of space, and is expected to be able at the very least to decode maps. The developing child cannot be said to be *constructing* or *inventing* an increasingly sophisticated code of her own; she is instead *approximating increasingly* to the social conventions of symbolic abstraction.

Feldman identified six levels in map-making development. The final level is the equation of the child's capacity with the conventions of map-making as normally understood. The previous levels represent different kinds of error. Some of these errors reflect conceptual difficulty, some represent the use of limited conventions. For the first three of Feldman's levels, the child presents trees, houses and other features as elevations rather than plans – and also demonstrates difficulty with scale and the relative position of objects. Right up to the fifth level the child uses concrete symbols or words to represent mountains: only at the final level can she use contours. So the child comes to utilize increasingly sophisticated sociohistorical resources – recognized conventional symbols – as her cognitive capacity develops (Figure 9.2).

Yet it is only by the exposure to those very symbolic resources the child becomes aware of the *possibility* for increasingly abstract conceptualization. The study of the development of map-making, even more clearly than the study of the child's logical thought or her moral thought, demonstrates the necessary interaction between a symbolic world – a framework of rules for representation which is part of the cultural resource – and the child's developing cognitive competence.

In practice, adults do not necessarily perform map-making skills at a high level of abstract symbolism, even though it may be presumed that they have the competence. The relationship between individual and social factors is demonstrated by studies of adults' representations of their home towns. These studies of 'cognitive maps' involved adults who presumably were sophisticated map readers; their representations however indicated two types of distortion. Firstly, they incorporated only personally salient features into their drawings, such as buildings of particular significance in their own lives. Furthermore they were inaccurate about certain physical features (for example the extent of the bend in the Seine) which they were clearly representing not from their memory of the 'official' map but from kinaesthetic experience of walking or driving. However, the cognitive maps were clearly not purely idiosyncratic; they had an interpersonal function. They may not conform to the abstract conventions of map-making; they did conform to shared symbolic representations which others within the same social group would understand. Here, therefore, is an example of the modification of sociohistorical, cultural norms or rules for representation to fit the requirements of the *interpersonal* domain, the utilization of a consensual convention which we can interpret as interpersonally generated within a group or sub-culture (Farr and Moscovici, 1984).

Normative–evaluative rules

The examples quoted so far are about prescriptive and descriptive rules; the third area of research is about rules for description, but rules which have an underlying *evaluative* element. This field is health, and the criteria for categorizing the states of health and illness. There are two studies that I will consider: one is the work of Bibace and Walsh on the development of children's understanding of the distinction between health and illness, and of the causes of illness, and the second is the study by Herzlich of the consensual representation of the same issue expressed by French adults (Bibace and Walsh, 1981; Herzlich, 1973).

Beliefs about health, like knowledge of the conventions of map-making, derive at least in part from the formal curriculum of school. All children learn about germs, hygiene and contagion, and have some basic understanding, by the time they leave school, of simple physiology. Thus the 'official' competence in defining health and illness does not include 'humours', or magical or punitive explanations of sickness, even though at other historical periods, and in other cultures, such explana-

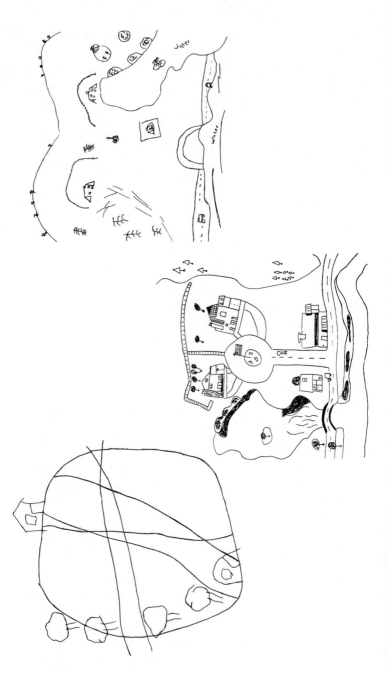

Figure 9.2 Stages in the representation of maps
Source: Feldman, 1980

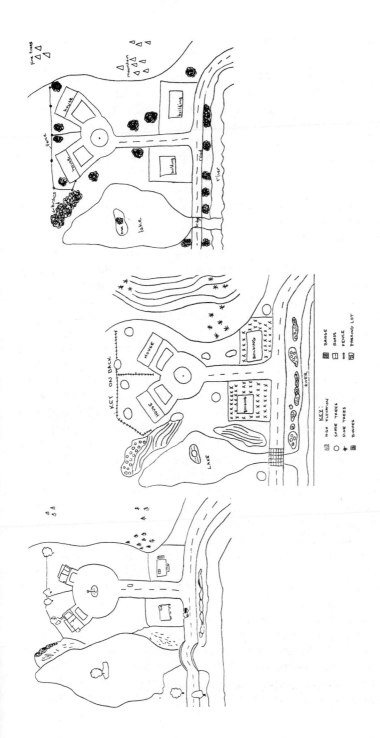

tions would be part of the cultural resource. In practice, however, Herzlich found that adults constructed complex explanations of illness which often contained a moral component, and that social as much as physical criteria defined the state of 'being ill'. Bibace and Walsh found that it was characteristic of children's developing understanding that they moved away from simple physical symptomatic explanations towards more socially defined classifications.

In the adult representation of illness and health, we see the sociohistorical frameworks which are the ultimate resources for the developing child's descriptions and explanations of illness. Every child experiences her own and others' illness, and it is through the *social* definition of *individual* experience that the child develops her own competence in representation. Herzlich found that despite the 'scientific' model of contagion and germs, adult French social representations were dominated by the idea of *toxicity*. This implies that illness arises from a person's way of life; central to toxicity are the idea of *pollution* and the idea of *vulnerability*. The toxic factors may be a consequence of external variables, like polluted air or chemical additives in food and water – or even noise – or they may be internal to the individual, like poor diet or the consumption of alcohol or tobacco. The individual has a personal responsibility for internal variables, and even external variables can be controlled by choice of where to live. Thus health and illness are at least partly within the control of the individual; there is a moral element involved. This is part of a prevailing notion that 'health' is a *reserve*; the individual's vulnerability to being stricken down by accidental illness depends on her responsibly maintaining that reserve in good order.

So, defining the boundaries of health and illness depends on a mixture of physical, social and psychological criteria. Having a temperature, pain or nausea are aspects of being ill, but more important are psychological well-being, especially 'being oneself' and being able to perform normal functions of life. The characteristic behaviours of a sick person – going to bed, social exclusion, the surrender of responsibility to others – are the socially recognized signs of a changed psychological state. For many people, being excused normal work by a legitimating authority – such as parent or doctor – is the primary criterion of 'being ill', overriding specific physical symptoms which may be in any case mediated by medication or by 'willpower'. One does not *have* to 'act sick', but if one does, others collude in the affirmation of the role, and the social definition of 'being ill' is established.

The social definition of illness, in which others collude, takes various forms. Illness may be destructive and damaging; it may be a temporary liberation from normal life, an enforced vacation; or it may be an active struggle, an 'occupation' in which the patient must cooperate with doctors in getting herself better. In each of these the social group, collaboratively enacting the social representations, plays a significant role both in the defining process and in the practice of the differing 'sick' roles – taking over responsibility, participating in the curing process, affirming the definitions and explanations of the nature of the illness.

The adult representation of illness is therefore a complex social and individual process involving explanation, justification and coordinated action, reflecting the shared understanding of rules and roles. The growing child, experiencing illness – her own and others' – participates in the enactment of the collaborative roles, and in the presentation of justifications and explanations of illness. This I would argue is a particularly clear example of Vygotsky's description of the social and interpersonal experience of concepts. The developing understanding of illness is the increasing approximation of the individual child's construction of the rules for defining illness to the social representation – the cultural resource – of the adult world. Bibace and Walsh studied the development of children's conceptions of illness. They interviewed both healthy and chronically sick children. From this they have produced a tentative 'stage' sequence of the progress of cognitive complexity.

At the very first level, the child has little understanding of illness. At the second level, described by Bibace and Walsh as *pre-logical*, the child shows an understanding of the symptoms that define illness, and her causal model of illness includes both the general idea of contagion and a limited concept of personal responsibility: 'I had a cold'; (why did you get sick?) 'Ronny gave me his cold'; (how did you get sick?) 'I went outside without a hat'.

At the *concrete-logical* level, the child understands that contagion has something to do with germs. She also has a concept that the individual may create the preconditions for illness through bad diet or through unwise behaviour, such as smoking. She understands that one is 'cured' through medication or specific forms of behaviour. At the *formal–logical* level, the child (or adolescent) expresses the same kinds of cognitions as the adults in Herzlich's study – a sophisticated understanding of the sequence of physiological events, and an appreciation of the role of stress and worry in illness. Like Herzlich's adults, adolescents are not necessarily *accurate* about physiology, but they attempt to express a rational and 'scientific' explanation, and to incorporate physiological, social and psychological factors in their accounts. It is apparent in both Herzlich's and Bibace and Walsh's work that in our culture illness *needs to be explained*, and that explanation in such terms is deemed appropriate.

The developmental dialectic

From the various foregoing examples, it is clear that there is a dialectical relationship between the *social representation* of rules which social psychologists have demonstrated amongst adult populations, and the *individual development of cognitive constructions* of rules on which developmental psychologists have concentrated. I argue that social psychologists have tended to ignore the processes of individual development, and have focused instead on the ways in which social groups collaborate in the enactment and articulation of collectively understood representations; these include explanations, legitimations and justifications. In contrast, developmental psychologists have – largely – considered 'social' processes simply in terms of the effect of dyadic or small group interaction as a catalyst in creating individual cognitive disequilibrium. They have tended to study individual reasoning in a social context, and the effect of interpersonal conflict on individual thinking, but they have not examined how the social interaction itself is a reflection of the wider social process whereby social presentations represent a resource, and a framework within which legitimation and justification of rules are prescribed (and proscribed). I argue

that Vygotsky's distinction between the *social (interpersonal)
interaction* process and the *sociohistorical* process is important in
understanding this dialectic. I draw the parallel between,
firstly, Vygotsky's 'social interaction process' and the kind of
interaction that has a catalytic effect on the structure of
individual thought, and, secondly, Vygotsky's 'sociohistorical
context' and social representations, which are the manifestation
of cultural consensus and the resource for shared understanding, justification and legitimation of rules.

This is the *logic* of the dialectical process in development, but
further data is needed to demonstrate how it operates in
practice. Such data is available in the detailed analyses,
reported by Turiel and his colleagues, of the interaction
amongst peers and between child and teacher. The studies of
Much and Shweder are also of particular interest; they specifically addressed the question of how cultural rules are transmitted to children through explicit and implicit forms of language
and interaction: 'We believe that it is more fruitful to assume
that cultural rules are continually tested, employed, clarified
and negotiated in microscopic moments of everyday life. These
moments . . . we shall refer to as *situations of accountability*'.
They point out that 'evaluative enquiries are ubiquitous in
everyday life. Demands for an account of why someone has
done (or is doing) what he has done (or is doing) occur so
routinely that they often go unnoticed – unless of course, an
account is not forthcoming' (Much and Schweder, 1978, p. 20).

Much and Schweder argue that what they term the 'cultural
message' is revealed in interactions, through the nature of the
sanction, the account given of the breach, or by what aspect of
the behaviour was singled out for comment. Through such
interactions, the child learns *which* actions need to be accounted
for (lateness, accidental harm) and what form of speech act is
legitimate in that situation. The accusation or request for an
account, and the response given to it, must reflect a shared
understanding of the situation. For example, A: 'It's ten
o'clock'; B: 'I'm sorry, I had a dental appointment' indicates that
B has understood A to be making an accusation, not merely
stating the time, that A knows B will interpret her comment in
this way, that B knows she should apologise for lateness, and
that B knows that dental appointments are consensually

regarded as legitimate excuses (whether true or not). Most is
implicit in that example; it is adult interaction, and adults can
take such consensual understanding for granted. Much and
Schweder's work shows how adults initiate the child into such
social representations by extensively spelling out the accusation, and by affirming explicitly that an account is legitimate.
Thus the child learns the rules of interaction *and* the rules which
have been breached:

Teacher: Madeline, we missed you yesterday. Where were you?
Madeline: My mother and dad didn't want me to come to school
  because they both slept late.
Teacher: O they had vacation yesterday?
Madeline: Yeah.
Teacher: Well, I guess that's a good excuse.

In that example, Much and Schweder identify the 'cultural
control message' as 'children are expected to be in school every
day'. This is the *underlying rule*, but also in this extract we can
see (1) the teacher asking for an explanation; (2) the child
offering two; first her parents' wishes, and secondly an
explanation of those wishes which she presumably regards as
legitimate; (3) the teacher's decoding of her reply into an
acceptable and legitimate excuse; and (4) the teacher affirming
to the child that her decoded message is accepted as legitimate.

The work of Turiel, Nucci and Smetana contains many
examples of such explicit asking for, receiving and legitimating
of accounts and explanations in young children (Nucci and
Nucci, 1982; Nucci and Turiel, 1978; Smetana, 1981). Their work
shows that children are adept at producing appropriate sanctions and invoking the correct rhetoric and explanation, both in
their interaction with peers and in their reporting of misde-
meanours to the teacher:

Tammy (to Agnes): I'm sorry, but you can't help.
Alice: She can help. You don't have to be just rude (pinches
  Tammy).
Teacher: What's the matter?
Tammy: She pinched me.
Teacher (to Alice): Why?
Alice: She wouldn't let Agnes help.

Teacher: That's not your business. I told Tammy to clean the table. I'm very angry that you hurt Tammy.

Alice, in this extract, (1) speaks; (2) acts (by pinching) and (3) legitimates her action and speech in terms of the rules of not being rude, letting others help and not excluding people. Tammy knows that Alice's pinching will bring disapproval from the teacher. The teacher responds to the message of both girls in her reply, legitimating Tammy but not, in this case, Alice.

These children, who are aged about five, already know what counts as a legitimate account or justification for behaviour, as well as knowing which behaviours are acceptable. They are already in tune with the social representations of helping and harming; they demonstate competent use of the sociohistorical resources of their social world. We can see in these extracts also the ways that teachers explicitly scaffold this learning process, through their own actions and through the explicit articulation of the rules and their justification.

Severally, Turiel, Nucci and Smetana have extensively investigated the development of children's understanding of the distinction between conventional and moral rules. These studies throw further light on how adult–child, and child–child, interactions convey a message – explicitly or implicitly – about the nature of the rule and the appropriate justifications for it. For example, parents adapt their disciplinary methods to the domain of misdemeanour; the child learns that violating different kinds of rules has a different kind of consequence. This applies not only to the actual sanction invoked but to the *style* of sanctioning. *Conventions* such as the breaking of adults' rules within the home are punished by power assertion or love-withdrawal; violations of outside-home rules – seen, at least by the mother, in *moral* rather than conventional terms – are punished by induction (reasoning with the child).

Turiel argues, 'Children experience social events that are moral, entailing *intrinsic* consequences, and social events that are conventional, entailing institutional systems of rules, authoritative expectation and organisation' (1983, p. 44). So the accounts given for moral transgressions are in terms of *extrinsic* outcomes. Nucci and Turiel observed this pattern with child–

teacher interactions in kindergarten and first grade; teachers gave *reasons* for their objections to moral transgressions, and they pointed out to the child the consequences of such transgressions in terms of harm to the victims. To conventional transgressions they invoked rules, sanctions and prohibitions.

As the child becomes older, distinctive adult responses to the different domains continue, but the pattern changes. With older children, teachers were less likely to respond to moral transgressions, and more likely to respond to conventional transgressions. Furthermore, the nature of the response to moral transgressions changed. Harm to the victim was invoked less often; teachers talked instead of *fairness* and *justice*. This shift raises interesting questions; are the teachers intuitively adjusting their level of exposition to the presumed level of the child's cognitive complexity, implicitly recognizing – and so scaffolding – the child's greater understanding of fairness and justice? Or is it that the teacher sees the role of the school in middle childhood as being to mediate justice and fairness rather than to control harming – in other words, are her own representations of her function different for a different age of child?

Interactions between children themselves indicate that they comprehend, and practise in action, the distinction between conventional and moral rules. Preschool children in fact rarely responded to each others' conventional transgressions, but when they did it was with a characteristic style of accusation and counter-accusation which did not involve soliciting the support and sanction of adults. However they did respond to moral transgressions; not by the articulation of charges of rule-breaking, but with an expression of primary affect – hurt or pain. For such moral transgressions they appealed to adults for support.

Older children responded to moral transgressions with retaliatory physical action, with claims of injury, or with appeals to empathy. These responses reflect the kind of reasoning that children of this age produce in discussion of moral transgressions – this would support Vygotsky's analysis of the relationship between interpersonal and intrapsychological experience. As children become older, they are less likely to call upon adult intervention, for either moral or conventional transgressions. Conventional transgressions meet peer ridicule or reminders of the rule; by middle childhood it is part of the social representations of children that the individual who transgresses is socially deviant (as for example in sex-role behaviour), and that rules should, *per se*, be obeyed: this is the message that teachers inculcated earlier in their lives.

Conclusion

In this chapter I have explored a three-part model of the development of the child's understanding of rules, which attempts to take into account the evidence from social and developmental psychology. The tension which currently pervades the interface between developmental and social approaches to social cognition arises from incompatible starting points; for the developmentalist, there has been a predominating assumption that knowledge is individually constructed, and that the interesting questions of development concern the structural transformations which mark the progression towards a fully abstract construction. For the social psychologist and the sociologist, the predominating assumption is that knowledge is socially constructed, that prevailing frameworks of knowledge and meaning shape the construction of individuals' thinking, and that changes in these frameworks result from a collective renegotiation in response to the structural pressures of social conditions or the needs of specific groups. The vitriol which may be encountered in critiques by one side or the other demonstrates the extent of the schism between the two sets of assumptions.

The schism has become less sharp as developmentalists have begun to explore the effects of social interaction amongst peers on the cognitive processes of individuals, and as social psychologists have paid more attention to the mechanisms by which the child becomes integrated into the social world. However, in this chapter I have argued that it is necessary to separate out the 'social' experience of interpersonal interaction within which the child specifically confronts the negotiation of meaning and knowledge in a face-to-face situation, from the 'social' world of social representation, metaphor and symbol which are the framework of cultural definition, legitimation and meaning. I have argued that Vygotsky's distinctions

between intrapersonal, interpersonal and sociohistorical domains provide a framework for exploring the differing processes by which the child experiences ways of making sense. I
have examined three aspects of 'growing into rules' – a
quintessential aspect of social construction and social cognition
– to illustrate the ways in which, by taking Vygotsky's
distinctions into account, we may be able to move towards a
rapprochement between the developmental and the social
models.

References

Bibace, R., and Walsh, M.E. (eds), *New Directions for Child Development*,
no. 14: *Children's Conceptions of Health, Illness and Bodily Functions*.
San Francisco: Jossey-Bass, 1981.

Bourdieu, P., *Outline of a Theory of Practice*. Cambridge: Cambridge
University Press, 1977.

Bruner, J., *Actual Minds, Possible Worlds*. Harvard: Harvard University
Press, 1986.

Damon, W., *The Social World of the Child*. San Francisco: Jossey-Bass,
1977.

Damon, W., 'Exploring children's social cognition on two fronts', in
J.H. Flavell and L. Ross (eds), *Social Cognitive Development*.
Cambridge: Cambridge University Press, 1981.

Doise, W., and Mugny, G., *The Social Development of the Intellect*.
Oxford: Pergamon Press, 1984.

Farr, R.M., and Moscovici, S., *Social Representations*. Cambridge and
Paris: Cambridge University Press and Editions de la Maison des
Sciences de l'Homme, 1984.

Feldman, D.H., *Beyond Universals in Cognitive Development*. Norwood,
NJ: Ablex, 1980.

Furth, H.G., 'Young children's understanding of society', in H.
McGurk (ed.), *Issues in Childhood Social Development*. London:
Methuen, 1978.

Habermas, J., *Communication and the Evolution of Society*. London:
Heinemann, 1979.

Herzlich, C., *Health and Illness, a Social Psychological Analysis*. London:
Academic Press, 1973.

Jodelet, D., Ohana, J., Bessis-Monino, C., and Dannenmuller, E.,
Systemes de représentation du corps et groupes sociaux, Paris:
CORDES, 1980.

Kohlberg, L., *The Psychology of Moral Development*. San Francisco: Harper & Row, 1984.

Leahy, R.L. (ed.), *The Child's Construction of Social Inequality*. London: Academic Press, 1983.

Moscovici, S., *La psychoanalyse: son image et son public*. Paris: Presses Universitaires de France, 1961/76.

Modgil, S., and Modgil, C., *Kohlberg: Consensus and Controversy*. Lewes: Falmer Press, 1986.

Much, N., and Schweder, R., 'Speaking of rules: the analysis of culture in breach', in W. Damon (ed.), *New Directions for Child Development, No. 2: Moral Development*. San Francisco: Jossey-Bass, 1978.

Nisan, M., 'The primacy of moral content', in Candee, D., and Kohlberg, L. (eds), *Recent Research in Moral Development*, Cambridge: Cambridge University Press, 1988.

Nucci, L., and Nucci, M., 'Children's social interactions in the context of moral and conventional transgressions', *Child Development*, 1982, 53, 403–12.

Nucci, L., and Turiel, E., 'Social interactions and the development of social concepts in preschool children', *Child Development*, 1978, 49, 400–7.

Piaget, J., *The Moral Judgement of the Child*. London: Routledge & Kegan Paul, 1932.

Riegel, K.F., and Rosenwald, G.C., *Structure and Transformation*. New York: Wiley, 1975.

Smetana, J., 'Preschool children's conceptions of moral and social rules', *Child Development*, 1981, 52, 1333–6.

Tajfel, H., *Human Groups and Social Categories*. Cambridge: Cambridge University Press, 1981.

Tuffin, R., 'The euthanasia dilemma: reactions of the press and public'. Unpublished BSc dissertation, University of Aston, 1982.

Turiel, E., *The Development of Social Knowledge*. Cambridge: Cambridge University Press, 1983.

Vygotsky, L.S., *Mind in Society*. Cambridge, Mass.: Harvard University Press, 1978.

Weinreich Haste, H., 'Morality, social meaning and rhetoric, the social context of moral reasoning', in W. Kurtines and J. Gewirtz (eds), *Morality, Moral Behaviour and Moral Development*. New York: Wiley, 1984.

Wertsch, J.V. (ed.), *Culture, Communication and Cognition: Vygotskian Perspectives*. Cambridge: Cambridge University Press, 1985.

Youniss, J., 'Moral development through a theory of social construction: an analysis', *Merrill–Palmer Quarterly*, 1981, 27, 385–403.

Name index

Subject index